William B. Spring

AMERICAN EDUCATION
Facts, Fancies, and Folklore

AMERICAN EDUCATION

Facts, Fancies, and Folklore

RAYMOND P. HARRIS
Director of Secondary Education, Mount Vernon, N.Y., **Public Schools**

RANDOM HOUSE   *New York*

Second Printing, January 1962

© Copyright, 1961, by Raymond P. Harris
All rights reserved under International and Pan-American Copyright
Conventions. Published in New York by Random House, Inc., and
simultaneously in Toronto, Canada, by Random House of Canada, Limited.
Library of Congress Catalog Card Number: 61–6258
Manufactured in the United States of America
by H. Wolff, New York

Preface

American educators have addressed themselves far too little to the nation's citizenry as a whole. Though the situation has of late begun to be remedied, the best contemporary writing about public education remains tucked away in the professional literature and seldom reaches the general reader. By no means surprisingly, therefore, public discussion of American education has been dominated, not by those most knowledgeably and immediately concerned, but by critics. And inevitably, a great many highly dubious statements about our educational process have been placed before the American people as the alleged "facts."

It is high time to expose these distorted concepts as the folklore they really are. With this aim, this book subjects a number of the currently popular notions about public education in America to closer scrutiny and measures them against what is actually happening in today's schools. Its focus is on the real teaching of real children by real professional teachers.

For the sake of the general reader, substantiating data

and bibliographic references have been kept to a minimum. In Chapter II, for example, only very brief mention is made of comparisons between the scores of present-day children on school tests preserved from other generations and the scores achieved by the children for whom those tests were originally prepared. Actually, educators have reported a great many such comparisons—and with results, it might be added, constantly favoring the school children of *today*. Similarly with the statement in Chapter VI concerning the great differences among the states in their abilities to support schools. Here again, as throughout the book, those who seek documentation can find it in abundance in the vast and excellent professional literature of American education.

In its basic viewpoint this book vigorously resists many of the currently popular criticisms of public education. Further, it takes a clear stand against some of the more general contemporary beliefs about American schools. And not least important, it argues as firmly as possible against the growing tendency to use our public schools as scapegoat in times of national distress.

Some readers might have preferred an even stronger case against the present attacks on our schools. And it must be admitted that in the effort to confine the book to a description of school practices that are more or less common and standard, a number of splendid educational achievements have not been mentioned. Since many of these newer developments have not yet become generally established, their proper evaluation must wait until they are more widely in use.

The author is deeply indebted to a large number of professional educators with whom he has had the privilege of working and from whom he has learned a great deal about the realities of American education. It is hoped that the views and experiences of these men and women have been described accurately and fairly in this book. The responsibility for all statements is, of course, solely the author's.

Anyone who undertakes to write a commentary on American education must do so in a spirit of proper humility before a subject so large and complex. In the pages that follow there are undoubtedly omissions and defects of presentation. Many important questions about our modern schools are bound to have been left unasked as well as unanswered. And most regrettably of all, not even the best of treatments of American education could do full justice to the magnificent accomplishments of America's hundreds of thousands of professional teachers.

R. P. H.

Contents

Preface, v

1. Facts and Folklore of American Education, *3*
2. The Fantasy of the Fixed Standard, *17*
3. The Myth of the Uniform Child, *38*
4. The Folklore of Discipline by Punishment, *59*
5. Imaginary Teachers Everyone Knows, *81*
6. The Anachronisms of Financing Public Education, *104*
7. The Unrealized Ideal of the Free Public School, *126*
8. Facts and Fictions of the American High School, *146*
9. What Has Happened to the Fundamentals? *171*
10. The Happy Plight of the Gifted Child, *190*
11. The Legend of Anti-Intellectualism, *206*
12. The Grand Illusion of Progressive Education, *223*
13. Those Maligned Education Courses, *243*
14. Scapegoating the Public School, *260*
15. Who Shall Decide? *276*

Index 297

AMERICAN EDUCATION
Facts, Fancies, and Folklore

1. Facts and Folklore of American Education

The schools today are news. They are spotlighted in newspapers and magazines, on radio and television, in books—in every medium of mass communication. Every citizen has been made aware of a whole range of school problems—from the need for more buildings (and of their cost), to the controversy over teaching reading, the adequacy of our technological education, and the opposing theories of training teachers. Education has become the subject of one of the Great Debates of our time.

This is not to deny that education has inspired a voluminous literature in the past. Thousands of professional periodicals and books roll from the presses year after year. Yet the public discussion of education today is in at least one important respect very new and different. What is written and said about education is no longer primarily directed to those professionally associated with it. The audience today is a far wider one. It includes everyone interested in our schools.

This enlarged and intensified concern with education

might well be cause for rejoicing. How to achieve the best possible schools is a question well worth talking about. And as with every other institution in a democratic society, the greater the intelligent popular interest in education the better. But, unfortunately, those whose voices are heard most often and volubly today are not professional educators—although some of them are rapidly becoming professional critics of education.

A great deal of the current writing on education contains generous amounts of an element I shall call the "folklore" of education. Such folklore, as is shown below, abounds in generalities, lacks reflection, is often without verifiable basis in fact, and makes no more useful a contribution in education than it does in any other modern disciplines. Professional educators, experienced in the actual processes and problems of education, have for the most part recognized it for what it is. Many others who merely write and talk about education have not.

Some of the most popular current statements reveal to the experienced eye the indelible imprint of folklore. Here are some of them: That our public schools ignore the bright student in order to concentrate on the dull one. That a bogey named "progressive education" has wrecked our school system. That children learned much more fifty years ago. That today's schools are persistently anti-intellectual.

I am sure that we have all heard these and similar remarks frequently. I intend in this book to expose such statements to the facts.

UNREALISTIC CONCEPTS

The folklore of education thrives whenever we view today's schools with yesterday's concepts. In a few cases, these concepts may have fitted the schools of days gone by—though by now their basis in reality has long ceased to exist. More often, these folklore concepts are little more than idealized memories that have never had any foundation in fact. And why, in spite of this, do many adults today continue to use and subscribe to them? Because, one suspects, they persist in seeing education not as it is, but in terms of the vague and romanticized images they retain about what school was like when *they* were children.

The folklore of education is bound to survive as long as judgments about schools are expressed by those who have little direct acquaintance with them. Yet these are precisely the people, unhampered by any first-hand knowledge whatsoever, who have delivered the weightiest pronouncements about the needs and ills of our public schools. Many of these people, some in high places, have spoken out as though from years of experience—when in actual fact they have not been near a classroom for decades.

The ignorance revealed in many of the comments of such critics is deplorable, but hardly surprising. How can problems that have plagued our educators for years be diagnosed and solved at a glance by people—no matter how distinguished in their own careers—who have no professional competence in education?

Most educators are more than willing to discuss school problems with anyone who is genuinely interested in improving public education. Nor are they averse to well-grounded criticism. For one thing, they respect the citizen's right to know what is going on in the public schools that his taxes support. And for another, they realize as well as anyone else that real improvement in public education will depend on better understanding of the school's functions and needs. Their door is always open to intelligent discussion and criticism.

THE GOLDEN AGE

Our society, like most others, indulges at times in the notion of an earlier "Golden Age," a utopia of the past in which everything is felt to have been finer and better than it is today. Any social institution, including the public school, can fall prey to this "good-old-days" attitude. And how understandably so! Reality is complex and difficult—in education as in everything else. It is more comfortable to think fondly of the good old schools. By now their numerous inadequacies have been forgotten. Their graduates include practically all of our famous people. And of course, their comparative inexpensiveness looks most attractive.

Not that there is anything particularly new about this. Americans have long idealized the public school, in part because of their devotion to such concepts as equality and freedom of opportunity. And though neither of these ideals has ever been fully realized in everyday practice in the schools, they have unquestionably played a most important part in motivating public support for education. It is a measure of the extent of our inclination to romanticize the public school that there have been some, even, who have sought to give it credit for all of the achievements of our civilization. This is, of course, so unrealistic as to be sheer myth. Yet it is also the kind of folklore that is difficult to debate. For no one wants to argue the negative position against such well-intentioned idealizing. Nevertheless, an educator must sometimes feel compelled to speak of facts, especially when the idealized schools are proposed as models for contemporary institutions.

The notion of a past Golden Age does our present situation no justice, nor does it help us in rationally coping with it. Rather, when the temper of the times seeks release, as it does at the present, the school becomes the target of all manner of attack. In comparison with its unrealistic but tenaciously-held folklore image, it appears wanting. As a result, of course, the idealization of the good old school of yesteryear is not only sustained but even reinforced.

As everyone knows, the Good Old Days were only partly so. But since our perception of reality is limited, and since we tend to remember our most satisfying experiences, it is not difficult to understand why Golden Age images persist. They are based upon merely a small fraction of the portion of reality that was actually observed. Moreover, since they are not obliged to remain consistent, they are easily changed to suit the occasion. In one moment of reverie, school is thought of as hard, rigorous, and exacting—an image useful in father-and-son talks. In another moment, in the company of adult contemporaries, the image is that of a light-hearted scamper through the school year. Today, high school is fondly remembered solely in terms of basketball tournaments and proms. Tomorrow, memory of the whole four years is focused on a single course in which a good deal of serious learning was accomplished.

SCIENCE IN THE STUDY OF EDUCATION

Meanwhile, the scientific study of education continues apace. Knowledge of schools and children is con-

stantly expanded and refined and our schools become
larger and more effective. Indeed, it would be difficult
to find a single problem of education that has not been
studied thoroughly and in which research does not continue. The verified knowledge of education is now sufficient to enable every community, provided it has adequate financial support, to maintain excellent schools.

Perhaps some readers will be reluctant to think of
education as a science, since the teacher's work with
students can obviously never be as exact as is that of
the chemist or physicist. Yet this objection can be raised
with equal justice in regard to every other social science. Whether it be economics, sociology, psychology,
or education, the concern of all of these disciplines is
with human behavior. And while fact as well as phi-
losophy may tell us that human behavior is ultimately
unique and unpredictable, there is no reason why it
cannot be subjected to scientific investigation to whatever extent our research and reflection may make possible. That this is as true of the science of education as
it is of the other social sciences is amply borne out by
our vast and growing professional literature in the educational field.

But the *science* of education, in the sense just described, differs from education's *folklore* in one very
important respect: it must strive always for consistency.
If it is to serve as a reliable guide to policy, all of its
findings and theories must sooner or later be brought
together into one coherent system. The process of building such a systematic body of scientific educational
knowledge and of planning to put its insights in actual
practice has been going on for more than half a century.
Revision in this has been continuous, with existing

principles and practices constantly being replaced by
new and improved ones.

Educational folklore presents a sharp contrast. Those
whose awareness of the problems of education has remained confined to such folklore thinking have not felt
it necessary to worry about intellectual consistency and
practical feasibility. In one breath, for example, they
insist that present-day elementary schools do not teach
children how to read; in the next, they demand that
our high schools increase both the number and the
difficulty of the books their students are required to
read. That this suggestion might involve an inconsistency—not to speak of a serious problem of bridging
the gap between inadequate reading ability and more
difficult reading assignments—appears to trouble them
hardly at all.

Thus our approach to education continues at two
levels: that of the science of education and that of
education's folklore. So different are these two ap-
proaches that they scarcely seem to refer to the same
schools. Often, indeed, they in fact do not. Generally
speaking, the professional educators are concerned with
schools that actually exist, while the currents of folklore
flow around schools that are to a greater or lesser extent
figments of the imagination. And since these two types
of thinking seldom meet on common ground, effective
communication between them is usually most difficult.

COMPLEX AND SIMPLE ANSWERS

The profession of education possesses a large and
refined body of knowledge to which a great many people have contributed. Yet it seldom feels qualified to

give simple answers. Viewing itself as a science, it has faced up to the fact that the problems it confronts are themselves likely to be anything but simple. The principle of multiple causation—that a situation is the result of a great many events and factors—obviously applies to most school problems as it does to everything else. The difficulties of children and their learnings are not amenable to any quick and facile solutions.

The folklore of education, on the other hand, is free to dispense with such intellectual rigors. Since its reference to educational realities is at best haphazard, it need not pretend to any great concern with a problem's full dimensions and complexities. Being the product of an all-or-none kind of thinking, it seldom feels constrained to pay much attention to the actual facts. Hence its characteristic specialty: the single cause and the quick answer—usually expressed in an extreme viewpoint.

If, for example, it is felt that the average college freshman does not know enough about American history, folklore simply proposes that another year of history should be required for all high school students. In contrast, careful study of this problem is unlikely to reveal any such single recommendation that will be useful for all students. For the fact is that some college freshmen already know much more history than others will ever know, while still others would never learn much more about the subject, no matter how many years they might be required to devote to its study. Though it may thus be accurate to say that the history requirement for some high school students should be increased, the matter clearly does not end there. Perhaps we need also to learn more about how to improve the effectiveness of our teaching of history. And undoubtedly too, we must continue to work on the motivation of our students. In any case, the problem is clearly too complex to be solved by simply requiring all high school graduates to take another year of history.

There is no denying that folklore may at times serve as a valuable cultural vehicle. It may even inspire heights of artistic and literary performance. But in most fields, charm notwithstanding, it has had to yield to realities and relinquish its power. We savor the quaint prediction of a hard winter from the thickness of the squirrel's fur in autumn, but we use the weather bureau's forecasts in making our plans for the weekend. Unfortunately, the power of the folklore of education has not similarly declined. Unreflective beliefs still guide far too many expectations of the public schools.

NEW OPPORTUNITIES FOR FOLKLORE

It is quite probable, indeed, that the folklore of education is at present actually gaining in influence. Modern American life is witnessing an ever-widening separation of adult and child activities. This contrasts sharply with the earlier periods of our history. As late as 1910, more than half of the population was classified as rural. The families that composed it worked their farms together and tended to live their lives together even after hours. The same pattern prevailed to a considerable extent even in non-rural areas, where the evenings at least were spent in the family circle, with regular contact between parents and children.

Today, neither the days nor the evenings afford much time for activities within the family unit. Much of the group effort that once surrounded the farm chores has disappeared as agriculture has become mechanized.

Many a father sees his children only briefly between his day's work and the evening's social obligations. At the same time, a host of children's organizations have developed to replace the former home-centered activities.

As a result of this widening separation between adult and child life, parents' knowledge of their childrens' experiences has steadily decreased. Today's fathers and mothers probably know less about the schools attended by their children than ever before. Many parents are not aware of the methods by which the elementary schools teach their children to read and spell. Some cannot even name the subjects in which their high-school sons and daughters are enrolled.

The decline in the public's knowledge of the school in recent years has provided the folklore of education with better opportunities than ever to flourish. Parents whose children are taught phonics daily in the primary grades have been known to ask, "Why don't they teach phonics any more?" Others whose children spend hours every week in voluntary reading have complained that their sons and daughters do not learn to read in the modern schools. One parent expressed admiration for his son's junior-high-school teachers but deplored the waste of time in teacher education. Obviously, the source of such criticisms can only be the well-known folklore of education.

50,000 SCHOOL SYSTEMS

There are almost 50,000 separately administered school districts in the United States. Each district is a school system in its own right, and each enjoys considerable independence within broad controls exercised by the state departments of education. Though federal regulation affects some districts in certain aspects of their work, as for example in vocational education, it has never been extensive. In effect, therefore, the public school "system" of the United States actually consists of half a hundred thousand separate school systems.

There are huge differences among all of these separate school systems. In size they range from the one-room elementary school and the two-teacher high school that still abound in many rural areas to the great and comprehensive city high schools that may employ as many as two hundred teachers. Differences in financial support are almost as great. Annual costs per pupil in American public schools range from less than $200 to nearly $1,000. And inevitably, variations in pupil learnings are no less enormous, both among different schools and within a single school.

Moreover, to these differences in size, financial outlay, and pupil learnings must be added the different purposes for which people send their children to school. Obviously, parental aims and hopes for education are not the same in a compact suburb adjacent to New York as they are in a large, consolidated district of villages and farms in the thinly populated areas of northwestern Minnesota.

Because of such differences, the American school "system" can be described only in the most general way. It is sheer folklore, for instance, to speak of the quality of learning or the efforts of students in *the* American high school, unless the observations refer to *particular* students and *particular* courses. Precise description is possible only with reference to specific cases. Yet much of the current criticism of public education has implied that we have a uniform national system of public schools.

In whatever form it may crop up, the folklore of education constitutes an element of grave potential danger, particularly as the growing public interest in education leads to demands for change. That danger, of course, is that important judgments about children as well as about schools will be based not upon our best knowledge of the facts but upon educational misinformation and myth.

Unfortunately, all too many decisions are being made on such inadequate foundations every day. For example, a group of parents agree that Miss Blank is an excellent third-grade teacher because she keeps such good order in the classroom—and in the folklore of education good order is equated with good teaching. Miss Blank's status in the community waxes as that of the other teachers declines. Some of them may even be tempted to emulate the methods that have brought her such good repute. And it may indeed be true that Miss Blank is a very good teacher. Yet the fact remains that no parent can properly judge her ability to teach by the orderliness of her classroom. This is only one of a number of criteria that determine her effectiveness as a teacher—and it is less important than some of the others. A great deal more must be learned about the situation in Miss Blank's room before her excellence can be confirmed and other teachers encouraged to copy her.

Let us consider what is happening to the children in Miss Blank's class. The parents have been pleased to learn that the children are kept quiet in her room. But they must go further. There are many ways to keep children quiet, some educationally more desirable than others. The best method, according to most professional educators, is to arouse in the students genuine interest and pride of learning. At the other extreme is the quiet classroom dominated by fear of disapproval and punishment. As many educators have observed, this latter is one of the least exacting ways of managing a classroom. It taxes the teacher's energy and ingenuity but slightly and fills the school day with unvarying routines of inflexible procedures.

We must also inquire what the children are learning in Miss Blank's class. Their academic achievements can easily be compared with those of thousands of other boys and girls throughout the country by means of inexpensive and easily administered standardized tests. Yet even the results of such tests would need further qualification. For they would necessarily omit still another important consideration: how does what is actually learned by her pupils compare with what they are capable of learning? After all, average accomplishment is as far beyond the reach of some students as it is below the potential ability of others. For example, Susan, a third-grader, can read as well as the average fourth-grader. This may well represent a splendid personal achievement for Susan; yet it is equally possible that she has a much higher level of ability and has been coasting through third-grade reading.

Nor would it be irrelevant to consider the question of how the children in Miss Blank's class are learning to think about one another. Though techniques of measuring boys' and girls' opinions of each other are not yet as well known as are achievement tests, it is possible to compare the extent to which individual children are accepted by others in their group, and even to compare the overall compatibility of one class with others.

The folklore of education judges Miss Blank solely on the children's reports of her ability to keep order. The science of education, in contrast, realizes the necessity of considering a great many other factors—only some of which have been here indicated. Because of its brevity and simplicity, the folklore of education enjoys wide appeal. Yet for that very reason it can never hope to achieve accuracy and reliability. These *are* attainable through the science of education—though only for a price. That price is careful study.

The Great Debate on American education has focussed national attention upon some serious problems of our public schools. In the near future, the citizens of America will have to make many decisions about such important issues as the education of teachers, new school buildings and equipment, teachers' salaries, the instruction for students of different levels of ability, and the number of years of schooling to be made available to all children. Irreparable harm will be done to American education, and thereby to the nation, if these decisions are guided by the beliefs of folklore. Mistakes can be avoided only by a more general understanding of the true facts about our public schools.

The folklore of education is particularly rich in the problems which arise in the learning of children and youth in the subjects which are taught in the schools. It will be the purpose of the next chapter to explore both the science and the folklore of education with respect to subject matter learning.

2. The Fantasy of the Fixed Standard

The folklore of education teems with sayings about the subjects children and youth study in the school. Since nearly all schools present instruction in terms of a subject organization, nearly everyone who has attended school has taken subjects in one form or another. Practically everybody can therefore feel qualified by personal experience to offer opinions on the amount of subject matter children should be required to learn. How much should be taught and when, have been very common topics for discussion in the Great Debate on education.

The most popular version of the folklore of subjects is that they must be mastered by all children. This is an example of the all-or-none kind of thinking which has been mentioned before. It seems to mean that every child should learn completely every subject that is presented to him before he is allowed to go on to the next level in it. Thus, fourth-grade arithmetic is to be mastered before fifth-grade arithmetic can be begun. Similarly, everything in the grades must be mastered before the child can be admitted to the high school.

Belief in subject matter mastery is less common among teachers and administrators than it used to be, because they see too much in their daily work with which it is inconsistent. However, it is still a common point of view among people who do not work with children in the schools. Presumably they are not aware of the contradictions that are involved in expecting the same subject matter learnings from everyone. Some of these contradictions result from the nature of the subjects and others from the nature of the children who study them. In this chapter, only those which are inherent in the subjects themselves are to be considered. The folk beliefs about children will be explored in the following chapter.

Underlying the widespread belief in subject matter mastery are certain assumptions. The most common of these are the notions that subjects are definite, that they are the same everywhere, and that mastery in them can be clearly determined. Yet all three of these assumptions are in fact serious misconceptions. The content of a subject is *not* something absolute. What is understood to be included in a subject may vary widely from place to place and time to time. And the mastery of a subject remains a very elusive thing to establish.

THE INCONSTANT SUBJECT

Subjects can be pictured more definitely in the imagery of folklore than in the schools where they must be taught. To say that high-school students should learn all of freshman algebra before beginning the study of plane geometry in the sophomore year would seem to be a fair statement of the subject-matter-mastery point of view. Each year of high-school mathematics is thus a pretty solid sort of package. No doubt algebra and geometry are very definite when parents see the words on a report card, and when they appear as units of credit on a transcript of high-school courses. They are definite also in the high-school's mimeographed schedule of classes. But close scrutiny of and full acquaintance with either course reveal only a roomful of students engaged in activities which are more or less related to mathematics. Most of these activities should consist of different kinds of reading, writing, drawing, and speaking, all organized about some central ideas of mathematics. Much of the subject's definiteness has disappeared.

At times there may even be some difficulty in distinguishing between classes in algebra and geometry. An interesting change in the contents of these subjects has been going on for several years, as teachers have sought to relate them more closely to each other and to other branches of mathematics. This is referred to as "integration," a term which kindles fire in the eye of the professional critic. Classes in algebra now apply their knowledge of such topics as equations and proportions to diagrams of triangles and rectangles, and the study of geometry includes the regular use of equations. Trigonometric functions are used in the solution of problems in both courses. Already, a good many high schools have discarded the conventional names of algebra and geometry in favor of titles such as "tenth-grade mathematics." Schools are quite different in the extent to which they have made these changes, but the notion of the constant subject is awkward in any case.

More recently, a number of other changes have been proposed for the content of public school mathematics.

These proposals would introduce more advanced materials than those which have been taught for so long. Such materials are now being taught experimentally in a number of schools, and probably their use will spread. As this occurs in varying degree and rapidity, the teaching of mathematics will be even more diversified.

To be sure, a visitor will usually have no trouble in determining whether he is in an English, algebra, or science class, but even in this he cannot always be confident. Both algebra and science teachers have been known to give spelling tests in the vocabularies of their subjects, and it is common for English teachers to test students on the spelling of the specialized vocabularies in their other courses. Such a word as "equation" would be proper on a spelling test in ninth-grade English, mathematics, or science.

The definiteness of any subject is further affected by the different amounts of time it receives in academic schedules. In a typical high-school course, if there is such a thing, the student spends about 175 periods in the classroom during the year. From school to school, the length of periods may vary from a little less than forty minutes to a little more than sixty. Even greater differences appear in the amount of time given to the course outside of the classroom. Some schools, and some teachers in other schools, discourage outside study, while others insist upon it. It is entirely possible for a year of ninth-grade algebra to consist only of 170 thirty-eight minute class periods, while in another situation the course may amount to 180 fifty-seven minute classes plus an additional two hundred hours of outside study. One must have a very high opinion of the abilities of the students in the first class to expect them to "master" as much content as those in the second.

The other school subjects are just as variable as the mathematics courses. Changes in the content of high-school literature illustrate the manner in which English courses have been revised in recent years. Many adults remember some of the literary classics which they were required to study in their high-school English courses. Millions of young Americans have been assigned the reading of *The Deerslayer, Silas Marner, Ivanhoe, Hamlet,* and *A Tale of Two Cities.* These were among the most popular of the required readings. Once, a college professor could be certain that all of his freshmen had had at least slight acquaintance with them while in high school. The secondary English courses of today are much less likely to require all students to read these books. *Silas Marner,* for example, is still a common assignment, but in many high schools it has been replaced by lists of other books, often classified by difficulty and by fields of interest, from which students may select their reading. In other schools, a more recent book which contains more appeal to adolescent interests will be read by the entire class. Stephen Crane's story of the Civil War, *The Red Badge of Courage,* is a widely used example. Much of the constancy of high-school English has vanished, but with it has also gone much of the time wasting for so many students who stared at the pages of books which they neither enjoyed nor understood.

PROCESSES OF SELECTION MULTIPLY THE DIFFERENCES

The variability of a subject becomes even clearer when the general processes by which classroom materials reach the student are considered. The areas of content from which teaching materials are selected are vast res-

ervoirs of knowledge. Each of the high-school departments is a reflection of the college department and the
graduate school beyond it. The high-school textbook or
course of study presents a very limited selection from
the particular reservoir of knowledge from which it
draws. The one year high-school course in biology shows
how much selection is necessary when its length is compared to an undergraduate college major of thirty or
more semester hours in biology, amounting to approximately one-fourth of the four years of college study. Each
high-school textbook, as well as each course of study, is
but one of a considerable number of selections which
may be quite different.

Further selection occurs in the teacher's use of the
textbook and course of study. The amount of time in
the course is one of the selective factors, for the year's
instruction often does not cover all of the material in
the textbook. Another influence is the interests of the
individual teacher, which bring greater emphasis to
some phases of the course than to others. At one extreme are teachers who make the textbook their only
source of materials; at the other are those who use so
many supplementary materials that the textbook is but
a minor part of the course.

All of the processes of selection are variables, although not to the same degree. Probably the amount of
variation which arises from the use of different textbooks is less than that which is caused by differences
among teachers, simply because relatively few textbooks
are available for any public school course in comparison
to the thousands of people who teach it. But surely the
combination of the three variables of the textbook, the
pressure of time, and the teacher's interests makes for
anything but constancy. A subject is not the same stu-

dent experience with different teachers in the same school, and the variations are even greater from school to school.

The varying nature of the supposedly constant subject can be illustrated by brief descriptions of the content which was taught recently in three American history classes on the same day in the same high school. Differences in the plans of the three teachers made the class experiences completely dissimilar for the three groups of students. In one class, the closing events of World War II were discussed. The teacher began by describing the German and Japanese surrenders, and continued with the problems of the immediate postwar period. The second class started with a student's report on certain phases of the economic role of the federal government; other reports were planned to consider additional phases of this topic on subsequent days. The third teacher led his class in discussion of the work and problems of the United Nations; on this particular day, some of its more serious cases were under study.

Obviously, this is diversity of content. It is much more than the variations in instruction occasioned by the weekly discussion of current events, for the work of each class was part of a coordinated plan of teaching. It should be clear, also, that the diversity is not at all a matter of quality of instruction. No one can say that the learning is better or worse because of the differences in content from one class to another. The illustration simply shows the inconstancy of subjects which is characteristic of the instruction in real schools.

THE VARIABLES GO TO COLLEGE

That the year's experiences in a high-school subject are enormously variable is exceedingly well known to the instructors of college freshmen. This is especially so in the state-supported institutions of higher eduction, which are frequently required to accept any graduates of their state's high schools who apply for admission. Perhaps the situation is different in the colleges and universities which can be more selective in admitting students, although the members of their faculties seem to share the same opinions of incoming freshmen as the instructors in the state institutions. Knowledge of chemistry among college freshmen who have had a year of the subject in high school will range from almost none to as much as is taught in the first semester of the college course. Some college freshmen actually know more about chemistry before they begin the course than others will know at the end of it. Nor is this situation unique to the subject of chemistry. Much the same spread of knowledge confronts instructors in English, mathematics, and the other college courses. Differences in individual abilities are responsible for much of the spread, of course, and the treatment of this topic has been reserved for the next chapter, but the fundamental differences in high-school courses which bear the same title are influential factors.

NOT ONE BUT MANY STANDARDS

The notion of a single standard of learning for a subject has the appeal of any simple solution to a complex problem. All that seems to be necessary is that students measure up to the standard before receiving credit for the course. In actual practice, of course, this would confront the teacher with some knotty problems even in one individual class. Applied to all of the classes of all of the teachers of any given subject it would involve truly immense difficulties. And before the prospect of its use in a large number of schools, the single-standard idea collapses altogether. Yet it is just this notion of extending educational uniformity over the whole country that the advocates of the single standard in education argue most persistently.

The plain fact of the matter is that the unavoidable variability of subjects precludes any possibility of a single standard of learning for any subject in all schools. The only concept that can be flexible enough to fit actual practice is one of individual standards for each teaching situation. Such a concept is a true image of what really happens in education, for every teacher has ample opportunities to exercise his own judgment in setting standards for the courses he teaches. This occurs at every level in education, including the colleges, and the differences in teachers' grading are well known to most students. They can easily be corroborated by simple tabulations of the marks given by the different teachers in almost any school. Some will be found to grade higher than others regularly, even in the same subjects.

The concept of many standards of achievement is accurate and adds to understanding of the schools. It destroys one of the basic myths of the folklore of education, and it threatens all of the unreflective beliefs that are associated with the idea of a single standard of achievement. The reality of many standards for learning is brought out clearly by considering the problems of classifying students according to their "mastery" of subject matter.

THE DIFFICULTIES OF CLASSIFICATION

If it were sound, the mastery point of view should help us classify all students into two groups: those who have mastered the subject and those who have not. The nature of the scheme offers only the two choices; every child must be fitted into one or the other. This proposition has the double appeal of simplicity and positiveness, neither of which can be offered by school people for any but the simplest of school problems. All that seems to be necessary is to establish the point at which students are to be divided into the two groups. This is an easy task in folklore, but in the public schools it is exceedingly difficult, for no single point can be used to separate pupils who have taken courses of the same title under different circumstances.

On any kind of measurement which can be used for the learning of students in subjects, the scores will seldom separate cleanly into two groups. Typically, they will range from low to high with some concentration near the center. At any point which might be chosen for the division, some scores will be just above and some just below. Shifting the point up or down the scale will bring others into positions immediately above and below it. The distribution of scores could not be otherwise when all of the innumerable variations in subjects are taken into consideration. To be sure, some scores will be so high that no one could hesitate to pronounce a favorable judgment, and others will be so low that no hesitation would be necessary here either. But between these extremes will fall the scores of most of the students, and it will be most difficult to be certain about any point of separation.

Chance must play a considerable part in the division of children into the hypothetical groups of those who have mastered the subject and those who have not. In a different school, or in the same school in another year, or with a different teacher, the decisions for many pupils would be different. The basic fallacy of the mastery theory appears in the attempt to apply a single standard in situations which are full of variable factors.

THE CONSEQUENCES ARE SERIOUS

To say that a pupil has or has not mastered a subject has serious consequences for him. In the one case, he can continue to move up the educational ladder with the others of his age group; in the other, he must lose all or part of a year. It will be unfortunate if such an important decision must ever be made upon differences of only one or two points in a final examination. The decision to hold a child back for a year should be made only after consideration of many factors, among which an examination score is only one.

The longer one thinks about the notion of subject matter mastery, the more dubious it becomes. On close examination, the apparently solid assumptions on which it seemed to stand so firmly dissolve into uncertainties. The subjects have little definiteness about them, so little that each actually amounts to no more than a year of experience in a given classroom with a given teacher. And mastery is virtually impossible to define as a means of distinguishing among the achievements of pupils.

Teachers have learned these things, partly through their own experiences in the classroom and partly through their professional courses in education. They expect a subject to be a different experience with dif-

ferent learnings for each child in the class, for this is
what actually happens in the schools. They teach, and
they test, and they teach again. One child learns more
from the first teaching than another can learn from several. The teacher has professional skills of individual
diagnosis and assignment which are useful in helping all
of them to learn more. In the exercise of these skills,
the folk beliefs regarding subjects are seldom helpful
and are often encumbrances. The concept of mastery
has little meaning when the teacher must plan instruction in literature for a student who reads at a level five
years above his grade. He has already "mastered" more
than most of the other students ever will. Nor does
mastery help in planning assignments for one who reads
five years below his grade and can never be expected
to accomplish as much in the study of literature as most
of his classmates already have.

No doubt there are many occasions in our lives when
it is feasible to expect uniformity of product. In many
industries, items can be mass produced to identical
specifications. Most Americans have been conditioned
toward this kind of thinking by their experiences in an
industrial technology. The attitude seems to lead to the
idea that the schools can turn out graduates as uniformly as a printing press can run off identical copies.
But mass education is not mass production, for schools
are not factories any more than children are inert raw
materials.

PROCESS AND PRODUCT

Process has a meaning for the education of children
which it can never have for manufactured goods. In

industry, the process is useful only as it contributes to the completion of the product. In human learning the process is often as valuable as a learning experience as it is in producing something. Playing a clarinet in the school band is an illustration of such a learning process. What happens to the student is at least as important educationally as what happens to the music. The boy who can never hope to become a first-rate clarinet player can still have a first-rate experience in playing the instrument. Product in the sense of playing music well is secondary to the process of educating the student. The quality of the education is even more important than the quality of the performance. Of course, this is not true in industry, for there the materials do not learn from experience as people do. This simply means that industry and education can seldom be compared meaningfully, and that any generalizations from industrial processes are of doubtful value when applied to education.

The folk belief in mastery emphasizes the product in education. The product may be a musical solo, a problem in mathematics, a written composition, a piece of furniture, or any one of hundreds of other items which are produced in school work. Too often, the mastery concept ignores the processes by which the product was was reached, and when it does it ignores the learnings that have taken place; yet the learning is the primary purpose of the school. Probably anything which youngsters can produce in school can be produced more quickly, more cheaply, and in better quality by adults. In industry, the quality of the process must be judged by its usefulness in turning out the product. The reverse is true in the school. There, the quality of the process must come first, and the value of the product is in making the process an educational experience of high quality.

School subjects lack the definite qualities which are associated with commodities. They do not have the physical dimensions of length, weight, and volume by which material goods are measured. Nor are they similar to the transactions through which merchandise is sold, for every transaction comes to a definite end. But no one can ever say that he has finished a subject, much less an elementary or high-school student. At best the freshman can take only a handful of algebra from the rich treasury of mathematics. The home owner makes monthly payments for years and finally completes the ownership of his house. The process of earning school credits may seem somewhat similar to acquiring a series of installment receipts, but the meaning of the high-school diploma can never be as definite as the meaning of a deed to a house and lot.

The graduate recognizes the difference when he says at commencement, "I don't feel the way I thought I would." His education is the best any country in the world has ever provided for all the children of all its people, but it does not have the definite, tangible qualities the folklore has led him to believe it should have. He has not completed a single subject, and very likely he has learned that he never will. But the folklore has not prepared him for the sudden realization that his education is so intangible. It may even have hindered his teachers in helping him to learn this. And the folk beliefs have not helped him to appreciate the values of the educational processes he has experienced in his twelve or thirteen years in school.

In most American communities, the culmination of a

public school education is graduation from the high school. The mastery theory of learning would make graduation one of the most important points at which youth are separated into two groups. It is a similar separation to those which are supposed to occur earlier in the school career whenever children are judged to have passed or failed subjects, but it is a greater and more final division, because it has more weighty consequences. For one thing, it marks the formal step after which the young man or woman may enter college to continue education. Or alternatively, it represents the passing of the milestone that makes him or her eligible for immediate employment.

FOLKLORE IN EMPLOYMENT

Graduation from high school opens several doors of opportunity in employment, in which it is common practice to require a high-school diploma as a prerequisite to the positions of greater pay and responsibility. In this respect, the employer seems to accept the diploma as the high school's stamp of approval. The tragedy of this very common practice is that success in the school often has little relationship to success in a job. Employment differs from school, so that many persons who have not done well in school satisfy themselves and their employers with the quality of their work. The two are different, for example, in the very important aspect of immediacy. Some jobs reward good work almost at once, while the final reward for success in school may be delayed for many years, and in some cases it is never received. School and work are often different in the nature of their requirements for success. The school emphasizes intellectual achievements almost exclusively.

Many, many jobs do not, and nonintellectuals often do very well in them because of their personal and social skills.

The influence of the folklore of education is shown wherever the high-school diploma is required for jobs which are primarily nonintellectual. Men and women who have not completed secondary school often find the requirement of a high-school diploma to be an obstacle to promotion to better positions. High-school principals run into many cases of this sort in which promotion seems to depend entirely upon the worker's possession of a diploma. As a rule, these are jobs in which specific skills in English, mathematics, or other subjects are either unnecessary for good performance, or have already been demonstrated. Naturally, the candidates for promotion are eager to obtain diplomas, but usually they cannot return to high school to complete the required courses. It is possible, in these situations, for an adult to earn a special diploma by getting a satisfactory score on the General Educational Development test. The theory here is that he has gained the equivalent of a high-school education in his experiences outside the school. Thousands of persons have secured diplomas in this way. The act of taking the test does nothing to make a person's services more valuable, but a satisfactory score makes him eligible for promotion. Why the employer has not taken the logical shortcut of giving his own test instead of asking someone else to certify an employee of long standing has never been made clear.

TOWARD REALISTIC TEACHING

Refusal to accept the mastery point of view has taken the schools a long step in the direction of realistic teaching, for it has freed teachers to do their best work in their own classrooms. Reasonable local standards can be set in full awareness of such important factors as buildings, equipment, amounts of time, and student abilities. The folk concept of a single standard for all can be replaced by specific, realistic expectations for all of the different settings in which real children go to real classes.

There can be little doubt that American schools are moving toward repudiation of the mastery concept. Forty years ago as many as one-third of all of the children in a school were apt to be behind one or more grades. At the present time, boys and girls are much more likely to be in the grades which are normal for their ages. Along with this trend has come an increase in the average number of years of school completed by individuals, so that all of the upper grades of the public schools now contain higher percentages of youngsters of the ages normal for them.

But learning has not been repudiated. The subjects themselves have not suffered. Students actually learn more subject matter in modern schools than their predecessors did. In the last decade, a large number of comparisons have been made in which pupils were given the same tests that had been administered many years ago at the same grade levels. Invariably, today's pupils have exceeded the marks of the children who first wrote on the tests. These results signify genuine progress, especially when it is remembered that any grade today contains nearly all the children of its normal age group, including some who would have been a year or more behind a generation ago. The results also demonstrate the fundamental inaccuracy of the folk belief in the better schools of the Good Old Days.

Much has been learned about measuring achievement in school subjects. Reliable standardized tests have been constructed for all of them. These tests can be used to define mastery of subject matter, but this is a minor purpose in comparison with their values in diagnosing learning problems. A standardized test will furnish a score for each pupil, and this score will show his achievement in each subject in relation to the achievement of thousands of other children. Whatever this may seem to lack in definiteness for those who think only in terms of mastery is more than offset by the accurate information it yields for use in teaching.

A local school system may choose from a good number of standardized achievement tests. Among the most commonly used are the California, the Stanford, and the Iowa series. These and others may be purchased by schools from the firms which publish them. In addition to scores which place individual or group achievement in relation to the performances of other children, the achievement test yields an Intelligence Quotient, which is the result of dividing the child's mental age by his actual age.

In at least one respect, however, the standardized tests are inadequate. One of the most important effects of the study of a subject should be the development of a spirit of inquiry. The ability to ask real questions is more useful than the capacity to answer simple ones. Achievement tests are efficient in the measurement of individual competence in answering questions and solving problems, but no one has yet devised a reliable means of testing a child's ability to ask good questions.

"MASTERY" INTERFERES WITH COMPREHENSION

The folk view of the school as a place where everyone is supposed to learn identical quantities of definite subjects on a uniform time schedule bears little resemblance to the real processes of education. It often hinders a person's realistic understanding of school. Educational processes simply cannot be fitted into a mental image of education as consisting only of mastering subjects. Two illustrations will show how inadequate the mastery viewpoint is.

Every person in our society must learn the attitudes and skills which are needed in social situations. Most of this sort of learning has been acquired before high school has been completed, and much of it is obtained in school. It does not fit into the conventional framework of subjects, although some of the learning does occur in classes. Most children go through about the same series of experiences in their relationships with others in their age groups. In their earliest years, sex preferences usually are ignored as small boys and girls play together in the neighborhood or in the nursery school. By the middle years of the elementary school, the sexes have separated into groups. The boys tend to play only with boys, and the girls only with girls. Rather strong and antagonistic attitudes toward the other sex frequently develop. Activities again begin to cross sex lines in early adolescence, although the timing varies greatly with individuals.

The characteristic activities of children undergoing these normal growth processes can be observed in every school. The fourth-grade Cub Scouts wear their uniforms to school on the day of their weekly den meeting;

the girls in the same grade belong to the Brownies. Before high school is over, most of them will be dating and dancing together. These or equivalent activities are normal and necessary experiences in growing to adulthood. Good schools offer their youngsters guidance through these experiences, but they are ignored or even opposed in the kind of thinking about schools that is limited to the mastery of subjects. Too often, children are expected to find their own answers to questions which they receive little or no guidance in recognizing.

To further illustrate weakness of the folk belief in mastery, let us examine the school's health program. This service usually includes health instruction, which is a very common school subject, but a good health program amounts to much more. Among the regularly planned features of a strong school health organization should also be physical examinations, health records, referral to family physicians and dentists, and provisions for emergency care in accidents and illnesses. Special arrangements may need to be added at times, as, for example, for mass immunization for protection against epidemics. This is not at all the same as the addition of another subject, and the folk beliefs about subjects are of little value in planning the school's health program. Useful incidental learnings undoubtedly result from the child's participation in the health program, but one can hardly speak rationally of "mastering" one's polio shot. Education as a discipline is not hindered in this respect, for it can as readily encompass Michael's need for glasses as his slowness in learning number combinations.

WILL THE SUBJECTS SURVIVE?

This chapter has not been written as an attack on the school subjects. It is not at all likely that subjects will disappear from the public schools in our lifetime. They seem certain to remain as basic divisions of the curriculum for a long time, although they will probably continue to be changed in content and organization by the same processes of revision which have been in operation for many years. Many new subjects have been added to the curriculum, especially in the high school, and some combinations of subjects have been made in both the elementary and secondary schools. Both of these trends will continue. Some subjects will undoubtedly lose in popularity as others gain. Probably achievement in learning subject matter will increase continuously as more is learned about teaching and as more teachers acquire more of this knowledge.

The folklore of subjects also includes ideas about the children and youth who attend the public schools, for subjects and children are closely related in all teaching. It is therefore appropriate, at this point, to examine the folk beliefs about the individual who goes to school.

3. The Myth of the Uniform Child

The most important thing for teachers and parents to bear in mind about children is that they are all individuals and, hence, all different. Anyone who has had any acquaintance at all with children cannot have failed to observe that each one of them possesses a unique combination of characteristics, abilities, and interests. Mary likes to read, and will sit with a story for an hour, while Jane almost never picks up a book on her own. Tommy learns an addition combination immediately, and remembers it the next day; Joey learns it slowly, after many repetitions, and forgets it almost at once. Larry is usually in the center of the group, and Nancy at the fringe. Gary flies into a rage on slight provocation; David seldom displays hostility. Mike is tall and heavy, John tall and slim, and Les short and slender. The outstanding fact is that they are all different.

In the recognition of individual differences, the public schools and the folklorists of education part company. Any institution which hopes to present a realistic program for all children must plan ways to do justice to the differences among them. It is necessary to provide opportunities to vary at least some of the details of a program to fit the children whom it is to serve. Schools differ greatly in the success of their efforts to educate children as individuals, but all of them make some attempts to do so. Folklore, in contrast, maintains the image of the uniform student. It is fairly safe to assume that anyone who talks about children as though they were all alike, or could all be treated alike, is talking folklore.

The differences among children are ignored by folklore expressions which suggest that all boys and girls have the same characteristics or that the same treatment is appropriate for all of them. For example, it is not unusual to hear that "Children are naturally lazy," or that "They'll all try to get away with something if they think they can." These are very broad generalizations indeed; they show no evidence of any serious thought about child behavior; and they ignore the industrious, responsible behavior which all children sometimes exhibit and some children nearly always manifest. Of course, positive statements can be equally erroneous. For instance, "He'll work hard if he wants it badly enough" fails to explain the actions of a child who has learned to get satisfaction from punishing himself and withdrawing from attempts to get what he desires. Practically everyone has witnessed such incidents of self-punishment at one time or another. The science of education seeks to find ways of improving such unfortunate behavior; educational folklore, with its sweeping remarks about all children, completely overlooks them.

The uniform student myth often appears in statements about the learning needs of children. A pronouncement that children need more spelling instruction may be impressive, but it is not very accurate unless it is qualified: certain children need certain amounts of specified types of instruction in spelling. Undoubtedly, some children do need to spend more time in studying spelling, but a good many do not. Since some of the weakest have very little capacity to improve, the reality of their need for more instruction is questionable. Many of the brighter children need less time for the study of spelling than their schools' daily schedules provide. Elsewhere, the universal need of children may be stated as more reading, more science, more study, more discipline, or more responsibility. Not only are all such statements inaccurate, but they obstruct effective teaching, for they ignore the real differences among children. If taken seriously, they would prevent diagnosis of individual learning problems.

CAN EVERYONE SUCCEED?

One of the favorite folklore maxims holds that anyone can succeed if he works hard enough. This belief is commonly illustrated with countless stories and verses about people who did succeed after overcoming great obstacles. Many of these accounts describe individuals with admirable traits, and they may be very useful as inspirational reading, but the basic underlying principle is faulty if applied to everyone. Accurate, useful thinking recognizes inequalities in human ability and differences in difficulty of the tasks in which success is sought. The addition of qualifying phrases will make our maxim more complex, and less quotable, but it will then describe more accurately the relationships between ability, perseverance, and success. The more specific we try to make such a statement, the more complex it will be. In a comparatively simple form, it might read as follows:

> Bright students can succeed at tasks of great difficulty if they work hard enough. They can succeed at tasks of average difficulty with slight effort. They are not challenged at all by tasks of slight difficulty.
>
> Average students must work very hard with little chance of success at tasks of great difficulty. They can succeed at tasks of average difficulty if they work hard enough. They can succeed at tasks of slight difficulty with little effort.
>
> Dull students can seldom hope to succeed at tasks of great difficulty, no matter how hard they work. They must work very hard with little chance of success at tasks of average difficulty. They can succeed at tasks of slight difficulty if they work hard enough.

These statements could easily be expanded to include more than three levels of ability and difficulty. They could also differentiate among various kinds of abilities, as well as different degrees of success. In a general way, at least, they constitute a fairly good description of the actual situations in which most teachers work. Teachers must deal with thirty or more children with different kinds and levels of abilities, different amounts of energy and perseverance, and different ideas of what constitutes success. In these situations, teachers attempt to fit children's individual characteristics into learning activities in which reasonable degrees of success are possible.

The all-or-none type of thinking which typifies the folklore of education may convert the above paragraphs into an argument against hard work in the school. It should be clear, however, that assigning a child a task he can hope to accomplish establishes conditions in which effective work is possible. Surely this does not prevent hard work. Instead it would seem to be a means of encouraging effort.

The great differences in the abilities of individual children may be illustrated by their achievements in any of the school subjects. In reading, for example, it is normal for some students to be at a level at least two years above their grades and just as normal for others to be two years below. The differences amount to a five-year span in reading ability within a single classroom. Often the span is greater. In one unusual tenth-grade English class, one boy's reading comprehension was at the normal third-grade level, while two others were reading at the level of the eighteenth grade, which is the first year beyond the master's degree. In another school, the achievement levels in arithmetic for 125 seventh-grade boys and girls ranged from the fourth to the eleventh grades. However, the majority were concentrated on the achievement levels of the sixth, seventh, and eighth grades. The achievement test from which the scores were obtained was given at midyear of the seventh grade, and the average score was 7.5. Since the average for this group was identical with the average of students from all over the country in the same grade, it is reasonable to conclude that this was a representative group of seventh-grade boys and girls— a convincing illustration of differences in abilities in arithmetic.

Many people have expressed alarm at the number of students who come out below average on achievement test scores. Yet to remain consistent, just as many should find grounds for satisfaction in the fact that an approximately similar number are scored above average. For by its very definition, the concept of average implies a distribution extending in generally equal numbers in both directions. Why should not the above-average be noted with as much elation as the below-average are commented upon with alarm?

Numerous voices from the past have suggested that the fifteen-year-old boy in the tenth grade who reads on the third-grade level should have been retained in the third grade until he was able to read fourth grade materials. Similarly, it is argued that eighth graders whose arithmetic is on the fourth-grade level should have been kept in the fourth grade. Presumably then, the two tenth graders who were also mentioned should be moved into the graduate school of the university, for they have shown their ability to read on that level. And the brighter eighth grade pupils should be promoted to the eleventh grade. This principle is suggested more frequently for the slower students, but it is equally unsound for all, since it ignores many other differences which in total far outweigh variations in a single subject.

It sometimes happens that an entire class is above or below the achievement levels of other classes of the same grade. For example, a few years ago the superintendent of a village school was confronted with a seventh-grade class which could not do seventh-grade social studies. The children simply lacked the abilities that were needed to handle the subject materials. However, they could do fifth-grade social studies fairly well. The folklore of education would probably insist that all of them be compelled to study the seventh-grade subject, or perhaps repeat the fifth and sixth grades en masse, but both the science of education and common sense would arrange for these children to study the materials from which they could learn the most without sacrificing the many other kinds of progress they have made in the school.

Individual differences in intellectual abilities are not apparent to visual observation. Nothing in a child's appearance gives clues to his ability to learn reading, spelling, arithmetic, history, or science. Often there are few clues in his behavior at home and in the neighborhood. Anyone who wishes to find the level of ability must make a diagnosis of the individual child. This may be done through careful and prolonged observation in specific learning situations. Yet the diagnosis can be obtained much more quickly and economically by the use of a standardized achievement test which can be administered to all of the children in the class at the same time. The scores will show each child's accomplishment and thus indicate his level of ability. His efforts to solve specific types of problems can also be analyzed. Learning tasks in which success is within reach, but requires reasonable effort, can then be planned to match his demonstrated abilities. This is the science of education in action. Nothing in the folklore of education corresponds to this sort of measurement, comparison, and matching.

Physical differences among children, in contrast with variations in their intellectual abilities, are more visible. Hence mismatching in this respect occurs much less often. One would obviously not ask a sixty-pound boy to lift a two-hundred pound rock. Nor would it make sense to test his strength by asking him to lift a weight of only two pounds. And though reading is not the same as lifting, and books are not weights, reading assignments can be just as absurd when individual differences are ignored. Since a reading assignment is not something tangible, its appropriateness or inappropriateness is less apparent. That the weight of the rock should be matched to the strength of the boy is obvious. And though less obvious, it is no less necessary that the difficulty of reading assignments be adjusted to a child's reading ability.

There is a further aspect of intellectual differences that may be illustrated by comparison with physical differences. Just as the strongest child may not be the fastest runner or the most artful dodger, so the best reader may have less ability than others in arithmetic or science. Each of the school subjects presents learning problems which are not wholly the same as for any other subject. It is true that bright children often do well in all of their subjects, but this can by no means be guaranteed, and occasionally a pupil of high general ability does poorly in one or another subject. Folklore might explain the discrepancy by labeling the child lazy, but those who work in education have no such simple explanation. They find it necessary to consider the many factors of the child's experiences in order to understand how he became the person he is in the classroom.

Public schools vary about as widely in their concern for children of meager opportunity as they do in all other respects. Indifference prevails at one end of the scale; at the other a few very fine experimental programs are in operation for such children. The Demonstration Guidance Project in the New York City schools is an example of the latter. Rich educational and cultural experiences were combined with intensive guidance services for several hundred youngsters from meager home and neighborhood environments. Excellent results were reported in raising levels of scholarship and reducing the numbers of discipline problems and early school leavers.

Improving the education of youngsters of limited opportunity is a problem in which public study of the educational opportunities of a community's children would help the school's program. Any improvement would serve humanitarian goals and would also be a first rate investment of citizens' time. And some improvement would almost certainly result from careful study and sincere efforts.

COMBINATIONS OF ABILITY AND OPPORTUNITY

The capacities for learning which a child brings to school are intricate combinations of his inherited abilities and the opportunities he has had for their development. It seems clear that children differ widely in the amounts and kinds of abilities they inherit from their parents. Yet what in a given individual is or is not purely native ability is impossible actually to distinguish. What the teacher sees incorporates the modifications that countless experiences have effected in the child's original inheritance. These experiences, if favorable, may have enhanced the original endowment; if unfavorable, may have deteriorated it.

There are large variations in individual children's opportunities for developing their native abilities. The scope of a child's experience is in some cases surprisingly meager, in others imposingly profuse. In one family, the children have had stories read to them from infancy until they began to do their own reading, have observed adults reading regularly for information and pleasure, have had children's magazines and books purchased for their use, and have been exposed to a rich and extensive vocabulary. In another home, the situation may be the very opposite: none of the grown-ups may have the habit of reading, no one may have ever read to the children, few reading materials may have ever been purchased, and the vocabulary of the adults may be limited and awkward. Where the best home opportunities are conferred upon children who have high inherited potentials, extremely bright prospects come to school. In those unhappy situations where low native abilities are born into the most meager of home environments, the resulting composite is barely educable.

Personal experiences may also lead to the development of specialized abilities. Through favorable opportunities a child can acquire early and unusual proficiency in swimming, science, the dance, and many other fields and activities. Yet by the same token, it is similarly possible for the environment to exclude contacts with some particular kind of learning and so to cause the child to develop less than his full potentiality in the subject in question. Of course, the extent to which favorable or unfavorable opportunities so affect children again varies with each individual case.

Not the least of the formative experiences of children are those which occur in the school, and these too are not at all the same for all youngsters. Even for students in the same classroom, experiences in any given subject are not identical. Both the differences in individual abilities and the conditions of interpersonal communication prevent any two persons from having exactly the same experiences in similar situations. Even though children read the same pages, work on the same problems, and listen to the same teacher, their learnings are different in quantity and quality. Whenever a student neglects any of the responsibilities assigned to him, the differences become greater.

Every conceivable combination of ability and opportunity confronts the teachers in the contemporary public schools. The differences in educability are great enough to create serious problems in the first grade. They become larger each year of school. Those who are ahead at the beginning usually learn more rapidly and increase their advantages, although some exceptions occur. This is a matter of common knowledge and comment among educators. It seems to have been overlooked completely by the folklorists in education.

EXPERIENCES, INTERESTS, AND BEHAVIOR

Much of human behavior can be explained by the principle that every person is the result of his experiences. This can be seen clearly in the classroom when a child is emotionally disturbed because of something that has happened to him. The influence of the disturbance may be so strong that it colors all of his actions. The child then expresses his unfortunate experience in his speech, his reading and, in fact, his entire behavior. Needless to say, children's actions and performances also express their pleasant experiences, but this is more likely to be taken for granted. Teachers thus learn a great deal about children's life outside the school simply by observing their behavior in the school.

Emotional disturbances interfere seriously with subject achievement. If the disturbance is chronic, even a bright child may acquire only a little of the learning which is expected of him. Where this is the case, the folklorist advice that he should be made to work harder has little value. The child needs much more to be understood than to be forced.

Not only in situations of emotional distress do experiences affect learning. All behavior is strongly influenced by the things that children have seen and done. In playtime arguments about cars, the child talks with his attachment to the family's model as well as with his vocal chords. The geography lesson is read with the family's vacation trip as well as with the eyes. Children think and behave with all of their experiences, both singly and in sets. At one time the parent's job shapes behavior and at another, the location of the family home. One set of experiences casts a pleasant glow upon the present, while another may be reflected in antisocial behavior. It is very probable that most children, even most adults, are unaware of the extent to which their experiences color their behavior. But a teacher must be able to recognize what is happening in all of these situations.

Just as past experiences shape behavior today, so present experiences will influence future actions. This is why it is so important that children have satisfying and enriching experiences in the school and in the home. The quality of the nine o'clock English class is reflected in behavior in other classes throughout the day and in later years. Children's experiences in each grade in the elementary school affect their behavior in later grades and in the high school. A child's dislike for arithmetic, for example, which originated in an early grade from some unpleasant experience, may endure as a lifelong antipathy to mathematics and even be passed along to his own children. In just the opposite way, a permanent interest in history may begin with highly satisfying childhood experiences.

Interest also affects the achievements of children. Ordinarily one who dislikes a subject is less likely to do well in it than one who is fond of it, for the liking is often the source of extra time and effort. No doubt many parents have observed that children who really like to read learn more reading by themselves than they do at school. A bright second grader who reads fifth-grade books at home and second-grade readers at school may actually come to dislike his reading class so much that he becomes a behavior problem. The teacher's real function must then become the direction of his reading rather than the detailed teaching of it. A child of equal brightness who has not developed an interest in reading may be below in achievement. Often interest is as specific as this, and its strength may be ascertained for a given subject. In other cases, interest is more general, and the child's attitudes of liking or disliking refer to everything in the classroom or even to the whole school.

To recognize interests is essential in teaching, for it helps match learning tasks to individual children. But teaching is more than recognition of interests—creating them is even more important. One child's interest in geography may be due to the fortunate accidents of earlier experiences, but the interest of the whole class in geography is the responsibility of the teacher. Of course, every teacher cannot be expected to arouse intense and continued interest among all pupils, for the intensity and duration of children's interests will vary as much as any of their other characteristics.

This is the point where experience and interest

come together. Children's interests grow from their experiences. In good teaching, experiences are planned both to appeal to interests already present and to develop new ones. Since children differ so greatly in both their experiences and their present interests, good teaching requires that pupils be treated as individuals, which contrasts sharply with the folklore of treating them as though they were all alike.

Not only is one child unique in comparison with others, but he is not even the same child in different situations. Personal behavior is influenced by the group of which the person is a member, so the child exhibits different kinds of behavior according to where he happens to be. He may be quiet in church and rowdy at the birthday party, the teacher's willing helper in school and a source of exasperation to his father at home. Undoubtedly many parents can recall incidents similar to the experience of the mother whose sons seemed to be fighting each other continually. When she asked, "What does your teacher say when you fight at school?" they paused to reply, "We don't fight at school," and resumed their scuffle.

One more point needs to be made about the way children differ in abilities, experiences, and interests. All of these differences are entirely normal, and they occur among normal children. Their total effect is to make of each child a unique person who has no exact duplicate anywhere.

DIFFERENCES IN STATUS ALSO

The folk conception of uniform students is quite different from real children who exhibit unique combinations of abilities, experiences, and interests. These

real children also bring to the school their needs to belong to its childhood society and to be valued as members of this society. Some children readily achieve such
membership, but for others it is difficult, and for some
nearly impossible. Most youngsters benefit from some
guidance in this important phase of their education.

Teachers can help children achieve status among
their classmates by creating opportunities for them to
appear to advantage. The occasions may be quite simple and fit naturally into the activities of the class.
Nancy practices telling a story to the teacher alone
until she can present it fairly well, then tells it to the
class. Her shyness fades, and her voice becomes clearer
as the other children show their appreciation. George,
who has not made friends, is taught to use the film
projector, and then asked to operate it before the class
"because he is so good at it." The next day he comes
into the classroom with a new friend with whom he has
watched television the evening before.

Situations such as these are easily contrived. They
open the way for children to earn respect, to make
friends, to become valued group members. George and
Nancy may be veritable jewels, possessed of sparkling
qualities ready to shine under the light of approval, yet
they are ignored by the other children. By providing
an opportunity the teacher says in effect, "Here is a
diamond! Watch it shine!"

Perhaps teachers have always done such things to
bring out hidden qualities in children. They are more
likely to do so today, however, because modern teacher
education prepares them to give the interpersonal guidance so often needed. It is a type of guidance which
does not fit into the folk beliefs about the uniform
child.

Failure to achieve status in relationships with others of his age group has serious consequences for the child. The effects range from withdrawal within the self to aggressive acts of open hostility. At the present time, the former extreme probably is more serious, because folklore often mistakes it for good behavior. While hostility frequently is misunderstood, at least it is recognized as being undesirable. When Little Brother is not included in the checker game, he upsets the board, scattering the pieces over the floor. This is his unconscious bid for attention in reaction to being left out of the activity. Understanding guidance would make him feel necessary in some other way, but most frequently, all he receives is a retaliatory blow from one of his older brothers. The most effective way to stop his interference with the game is to help him earn the attention and respect he needs, perhaps by teaching him the game.

COMPETITION AND COOPERATION

Some knowledge of individual differences among children is invaluable in understanding the place of competition in the school. In general, the folklore of education tends to overemphasize the values of competition in learning activities. The common essay and poster contests are examples of the point of view which regards all children as uniformly eager to compete on every occasion. To some extent the viewpoint is realistic. Children often like to compete against one another, and a great deal of competition looms ahead for them in life. But, in addition, they will encounter many situations in which they must cooperate with other people. The learning activities of the school must provide experiences in cooperation as well as competition. Neither should be eliminated, but neither should be over-emphasized at the expense of the other.

Wholesale competition in the school is objectionable because it treats as though they were alike children who are different. Constructive competition requires equality or near-equality among those involved. But even near-equality is lacking in the ordinary classroom. There are such great differences that only a few children have any chance to win. The number of potential winners can be increased slightly by changing the nature of the contests from time to time, but it will still include only a minority of the class. Children know this, of course, and act upon their knowledge. The most common of all forms of competition in the school is for grades, which has ceased to be a real contest for most of the students at an early age. They have learned that they cannot get the top grades, and they no longer strive for them. A public school in which every child seeks to lead his class is fictional. A reasonable degree of conformity is the rule, and actual competition from everyone is the mark of the exceptional class. Genuine interest in learning is a much more effective motivating force than competition for grades.

Competition among students does appear to provide incentives for them. A reading contest should stimulate them to want to read and a spelling bee should create interest in spelling. One may question whether this sort of incentive is worth very much, however, because it is an artificial inducement having no real connection with the activity it stimulates. In the long run, the competition may actually be harmful. If children read to win a contest, they are apt to stop reading as soon as the prize has been awarded. The stimulated interest in spelling may not survive beyond the duration of the spelling bee.

Better incentives are to be found within the activity it-self, and these are the incentives upon which permanent interests are built. Those who read because they have learned to want to read are more likely to continue their interests into adult life than those who read to win prizes.

The idea that competition in the school always has values did not originate in the school. That is one of the reasons it is folklore. It represents an attempt to solve school problems by the use of procedures which are in play outside the school. The classroom, however, is not a ball park or a boxing arena, nor is it the world of busi-ness. Only a moderate amount of competition is benefi-cial to learning experiences.

The activities of daily living present everyone with many needs for working harmoniously with other peo-ple. The home, the neighborhood, the church, and the community abound with such cooperation. Even in the business world people must work together. Yet the folk-lore of education pays no attention to the values of learning cooperation in the school. Oddly, parents who visualize their children as competing eagerly in school, seldom expect to compete very seriously with one an-other in their Parent Teachers Associations.

Competition in the school reaches its peak in inter-scholastic athletics, which receive more publicity than all of the other school activities combined. The pictures of the senior honor students appear in the local news-paper once in the spring of the year, but basketball makes the sports page every day for months. All high-school students are enrolled in English classes which are seldom publicized. A handful of boys on the athletic team get headlines several times a week. In all except the smallest high schools, athletic competition is limited to a small percentage of the students; the great majority never have the opportunity to play for their schools in a single game in any sport. In the tiny high schools which still exist in a few rural states, all of the boys can be on the basketball squad, and all of the girls can be cheerleaders. In the larger high schools in the cities, which enroll hundreds and even thousands of students, twenty or thirty boys compete for their school in basketball. The only role left for the others is that of spectator, a role which many do not care to accept. If athletic competition is ever to realize the values which are claimed for it, and which often benefit the limited numbers of participants, surely something should be done to enable more students to share in these benefits.

NO MINIMUM ESSENTIALS

Many people approve of the idea of grade-by-grade lists of minimum learnings, because it seems to offer a way to establish regularity in the children's progress through school. The plan would assign definite content to be studied in each subject in each grade, and every child would be required to learn these contents before being promoted. Teaching should be simplified under such an arrangement, since all children entering any particular grade could be presumed to know the minimum essentials of all of the earlier years. The advantages seem to be so obvious, and the plan so simple, that the idea has become quite popular.

Essentially, of course, it is a variation of the fixed standards concept. The differences are only in the choice of words. The standards for each level of each subject are to be defined as "mastery" of the minimum essentials. Even if the school subjects were definite enough to permit belief in the theory of fixed standards, the known facts of individual differences among children would render such a plan unfeasible. Whether proposed as fixed standards or as minimum essentials, the concept could only apply to an imaginary school attended by uniform children.

Real schools, which must plan instruction for all levels of ability, would need to prepare many different lists of minimum learnings to accommodate the educabilities of all their pupils. The fundamental meaning of "least" would then be removed from the term "minimum," and the idea would lose its definiteness and simplicity. If only one list were to be prepared, it would need to be set so low that it would be no test at all of the learning of the majority, or so high that a great many could not hope to accomplish it.

The values which may be anticipated from minimum essentials as teaching guides can be realized from two other very common instructional aids. One is the "course of study" for the high-school subject or for the elementary grade. This is available to practically all teachers. It is their state department of education's official outline of the content that is to be taught. The larger city school systems usually have their own local courses of study to supplement those which have been published by the state departments. The second guide, which is available to every teacher, is the textbook for the course. Most modern textbooks contain comprehensive, well-organized treatments of their subjects. So often have they been written to conform to state courses of study that this is a regular feature in advertising and promoting them. The teacher who needs to be guided in what to teach and when to teach it, as beginners often do, can follow the course of study and the textbook with full confidence that they include the essentials of the subject.

Intermingled with the folklore of students are many beliefs about the place of authority and discipline in the school. The whole topic of authority and discipline is so important in public education that it should receive full attention. Chapter IV will consider the folklore of discipline in comparison with some of the learnings that have been achieved in the scientific study of children.

4. The Folklore of Discipline by Punishment

Discipline in schools is an ever-popular topic. Its inherent aspects of conflict and violence have infinitely more audience appeal than do the less dramatic routines of daily instruction. Misbehavior and punishment are more interesting to most of us than is the teaching of subtraction or the use of the comma. Breaches of discipline can always spark a conversation or an editorial. Even among teachers there is a tendency to emphasize discipline out of all proportion to its actual place in their work. A single act of misbehavior and punishment is often good for more hours of shop talk than an entire week of satisfactory conduct by a whole class. Disciplinary problems have even become the subject of saleable fiction.

On the other hand, discipline has also been thoroughly investigated by educators and others who work with young children. Novels and short stories of violence in the schools are far outnumbered by the serious books and magazine articles on the problems of student behavior. Excellent reading materials abound for anyone who wishes to study discipline in the schools.

As one might expect, the popular treatment of discipline is replete with folklore-type thinking. The concept of the uniform child appears frequently, not in the sense of actual behavior, but in the ideal of the well-mannered student. Implied in this ideal is an authority-subordinate relationship in which the teacher is viewed as the authority, and the child the subordinate. This is customarily expressed in such phrases as "respect for authority," "toe the mark," and "make them mind." And as far as the deviating student is concerned, folklorist thinking sees only one effective remedy: punishment.

Essentially this is a negative viewpoint, for it defines discipline in terms of what children should not do, instead of what they should do. The "Don't talk, don't move" approach to the direction of behavior obscures the school's real purposes of helping children learn to do things. Teachers can be more effective by beginning with the children's learning needs and then trying to organize the kinds of behavior that will be most likely to serve these needs. This is what positive methods of discipline do: they establish order in the classroom by concentrating pupil attention on interesting and useful activities.

Public attention to discipline is always appropriate but it is not useful as long as it is guided by folk beliefs. Here, as in so many other issues in education, misunderstanding makes no contribution, and often interferes with constructive efforts to maintain satisfactory pupil behavior. The facts of education can lead to a far better understanding of discipline in the public schools. First, however, we must abandon slogan-talking and consider some very complex problems of human behavior.

The behavior of a child of preschool age will illustrate the source of some of the disciplinary problems of children. At a birthday party for an eight-year-old boy, whose four-year-old brother also attended, one of the games required each contestant, while blindfolded, to pick up three potatoes in a line and carry them to the other end of the room. Everything in the potato race was within the abilities of the eight-year-olds who were present; they scrambled through the game, some more successfully than others. Cheering and advice from the nonparticipants added to the excitement. But the simple physical coordinations the game required were beyond the abilities of the four-year-old brother. As fast as he picked up one potato, he dropped another. Suddenly he stood up, still blindfolded, and hurled a potato across the room. He stooped for another and threw it. Then he began to cry and swing his fists.

The child's performance was a four-year-old version of the "berserk" battle frenzy of Norse folklore, except that he was not as invulnerable as the warriors of mythology. The adult who was present picked him up and carried him, screaming and struggling, from the room.

Here is an opportunity to test one's ideas of discipline for children by considering how to treat this unhappy four-year-old. His conduct was unacceptable, even at a noisy birthday party for boys. Should the child be punished? Or would some other treatment be more appropriate?

NONRATIONAL BEHAVIOR

The child's behavior was completely nonrational. For one thing, he did not remove the blindfold before he began to throw and strike. For another, his hostility was not directed at any target; he neither threw at, nor hit at, anyone. His response was one of blind aggression —he was frustrated because he could not do what was expected of him. Had he been older, the response might have been less violent; he might simply have refused to enter another game.

Sometimes disciplinary problems in the school come about in much the same way. Frustrated because they cannot do the assigned tasks, children respond to their frustration with aggression. Their actions are nearly always milder than those of the four-year-old, although occasionally a real explosion does occur. When the response is negative—refusal to participate—the child is likely to be called shy. But frequently children who are shy in the classroom are not the same in their home and play activities. Sometimes the nonparticipants in the school are not recognized as such and are thought of as good, even as model, children.

Whenever children are asked to read, or spell, or work problems beyond their abilities, frustration is nearly inevitable. And from frustration is generated aggression. Below average, but normal children experience tremendous amounts of frustration in their school years. They miss twenty of the fifty words on the spelling test or get only half of the problems right in arithmetic. They also get more than their share of punishment. It is not surprising that so many of them drop out of the school as soon as they reach legal school-leaving age.

Folklore demands that we punish the frustrated child whose noisiness and rudeness, resulting from his frustration, offend the mannerly, responsive folklorist ideal. Yet his rudeness has in this case been nothing but a symptom of underlying emotional disturbance. His actions were nonrational; he did not know the real cause of his misbehavior. It is therefore no more logical to punish *in this situation* than to punish a child for having a fever. Indeed, punishment is wholly out of place here, for its net effect is likely to be little more than to make the child conceal his responses in apparent conformity, or else to make him more obstreperous than before.

Punishment never helped anyone succeed at a task that was completely beyond his reach. No amount of scolding will enable a child to read when he does not know how. Moreover, punishment of this kind is unfair, for the real error is the adult's, who mismatched the task to the child's abilities.

Probably the most common error teachers and parents make in working with behavior problems is to treat misconduct generated by frustration as though it were deliberate willfulness. Misbehavior among children is so often nonrational that the typical answer of, "I don't know" to the adult's query of, "Why did you do it?" is frequently the correct answer. The unhappy child actually does not know why he misbehaved. Probably almost as often, the exasperated adult does not really know either.

TREATING THE CAUSES

A much more effective way of dealing with disciplinary problems of frustrated children is to assign them learning tasks at which they can succeed, that is, to remove the real causes of misbehavior instead of punishing the symptoms. The four-year-old, given games at which he can succeed, is not likely to go "berserk," for success will motivate him to behave according to group expectations. Much the same thing can happen in any classroom when learning materials are matched to the known abilities of the pupils.

But frustration does not arise from lack of ability alone. Persons quickly become frustrated from disinterest. Many a youngster resents academic assignments because his greatest concern is to earn money for his family or for himself, or because his keenest desire is to raise his personal standing among the others in his age group. This kind of frustration is especially evident in the secondary grades, and often leads to undesirable behavior. Punishment in such instances may be expected to engender greater dislike of the school. Rarely will it bring about real improvement in attitudes.

It is true that punishment ordinarily relieves the angry feelings of the adult who administers it, and this is probably its only real value in those cases where frustration has been responsible for misbehavior. This is scarcely a defensible reason for punishing. A brisk walk around the block should relieve a harassed adult just as effectively.

Preschool behavior will furnish another informative example of misconduct and its treatment. A father came home from work late one afternoon to find his three-year-old son "howling around the house." There had been no afternoon nap that day; it was nearly dinnertime; and Timmy was tired, hungry, and cross. Perhaps the father shared these feelings so near the close of the day, but the responsibility to resolve this situation was his, not the child's. A brisk spanking would have been the folk method of handling Timmy, but it would not have given him the rest, food, and tranquillity he needed so badly. A certain type of "modern" parent might have attempted to reason the child out of his emotional state. But this father did neither; he simply held out his arms and said, "Timmy, you haven't given me a hug all day." In a flash the angry, howling behavior changed to affection as the child rushed into his father's arms. The little boy needed sympathetic understanding, and he got it. Adults who work with the many angry, confused teen-agers who attend today's high schools need to learn more about the equivalent of this father's hug.

BUILDING DESIRABLE RELATIONSHIPS

Permanent relationships between adults and children are created and sustained by their actions toward each other. Every show of understanding by the adult strengthens the child's confidence in him; every act of indiscriminate punishment, on the other hand, establishes the child more firmly in the position of subordinate. To some extent a subordinate position is necessary for younger children. Yet in our society at least, it cannot be regarded as a satisfactory foundation for adult life if it is the only relationship the child experiences. If he is to attain full stature as an adult citizen he must sooner or later outgrow the subordinate role. An adult-child relationship based on mutual understanding can grow into a mature relationship among adults.

At times of course, deliberate misbehavior does happen. In such cases punishment is appropriate, and it is possible to err by failure to punish. When a child knows he is being naughty, even going so far as to challenge adults by his acts, he should expect to be corrected, as he very likely does. Not punishing willful misbehavior may even be confusing to the child, for the omission fails to confirm his understanding of what is proper, and it actually weakens his confidence in adult guidance.

At other times, adults must exercise a police function in order to protect other persons or valuable property. Some behavior is so outrageous that it must be stopped at once, no matter what its underlying reasons. A child who has matches and lights fires must be restrained in the interests of general safety. However, the police function is rarely necessary in any normal group of children, just as it is seldom needed for most adults. The need for such action occurs about as often among a class of thirty children as it does among their parents. And even when circumstances demand prompt action, they need not lead to immediate punishment, though they should be the signal for careful study of the real causes of the misconduct. Teachers and policemen alike are more effective when they prevent violent behavior than when they punish it.

It should by now be clear that no universal rules can be formulated for dealing with the behavior problems of children. The folklore of quick and inevitable punishment is easy but inadequate. Understanding and consideration are essential to the effective treatment of behavior problems.

THE ORDERLY CLASSROOM

Most people, when they speak of discipline, have in mind orderly conduct. Actually, however, the most orderly conduct is found in classes where the teacher seems to give little or no attention to the matter. The best school discipline results from interest and accomplishment. Very few children misbehave when they are succeeding at something they want to do. The unruly classroom, or home, is the one in which negative commands and punishments are used freely. Such circumstances often degenerate into contests of will between adults and children. At this point discipline has already failed, for no adult can hope to excel all children in will power any more than in loudness of voice, physical strength, or intelligence. The notion of the teacher who wins all the arguments calls for more volitional stamina than most people possess and ignores the fact that the argument begins when real discipline has failed.

WHO MISBEHAVES?

It is apparent, from records of disciplinary offenses, that the majority of them are committed by a small number of pupils. A great many children go through the school year without any noticeable misconduct, while a small minority are habitual offenders. Many youngsters attend high school for four years and graduate without ever having been sent to the principal's office to be disciplined. Others are sent out of class regularly. In this, the school situation is much like the adult world, where most persons are law-abiding, and only a small number break the laws. Critics of the schools have tended to ignore the patterns of majority behavior to concentrate their remarks upon the conduct of the minority of students who violate the school's regulations. The repeaters are worthy of critical attention, not for the purpose of condemning the school's discipline, but to judge the effectiveness of trying to cope with them through punishment.

The theory of discipline by punishment gets its most thorough application in the handling of the school's regular offenders. They are scolded, sent to the principal's office, kept after school, assigned extra work, suspended from classes, and occasionally whipped, but their misbehavior continues in spite of the punishment. This should raise some serious doubts on the matter. For if the same child is being spanked every day for the same offense, it is time to ask whether the spanking is doing any good.

CHILDREN BRING MISCONDUCT TO SCHOOL

Whenever misbehavior cannot be changed by the best efforts of teacher and principal, the most probable reason is that the source of the misconduct is outside the school. These are the most serious problems of discipline. Teachers are virtually powerless in working with them, because they have no control over the causes of the misbehavior. One high-school boy who was rude and insulting to teachers and fellow-students came to the school nearly every morning charged with aggression because of events that had happened at home. His school experiences merely triggered explosions directed at whatever persons happened to be near him. Nothing within the power of the school could improve the home, hence none of the school's efforts improved his conduct more than temporarily.

Unsatisfactory as the boy's behavior was in the school, it was still better than in his home. In this respect his case was not unusual, for many parents permit conduct at home which they would censure severely if it occurred in the school. Perhaps this is not a very logical point of view, but it is quite common, and well worth thoughtful consideration: Is it really fair to expect the school to maintain higher standards of behavior than those which are accepted in the home and in the community?

WHAT CAN THE SCHOOL DO WITH THE INCORRIGIBLES?

The presence of incorrigible children is an exceedingly unpleasant reality in many public schools today. These youngsters do not respond to any of the procedures devised by teachers and specialists in behavior problems. Parents and community officials have experienced the same failures in their work with these children. Frequently, they disrupt the continuity of the educational program. Their achievements are usually so slight as to be without value either to themselves or to anyone else.

The incorrigibles cannot be dismissed from the school the way an employer can discharge unsatisfactory employees. While the law protects our children's privilege to attend public school, it also shelters chronic misbehavers from the consequences of all but their most serious acts. Nor are they permitted voluntarily to leave the school, even though they may be truant more often than they are in attendance. The result is the continuing and exasperating presence of a small number of students over whom no one has any real control.

The folklore of education places more responsibility for student conduct upon the school than is realistic in American life in the middle years of the twentieth century. Many functions which were performed by the family in earlier periods of our history have been transferred to the school. At one time children were expected to receive from the school only their formal education. The family provided for their health, protection, vocational training, and recreation. Today's schools teach more subjects, and also perform many other previously family functions for children.

In the old days, families were responsible for getting their children to school, for feeding them, and for protecting their health. The sons learned farming, or other trades, from their fathers or in an apprenticeship; the daughters were taught housekeeping tasks by their mothers. Schools now exercise some or all of these functions. Some children today cross the streets on their way to school under the protection of the safety patrol which has been organized by the school. Some of the others are picked up at home or at a nearby waiting point and brought to the school by bus. All of them often receive health inspections and immunization shots at the school. Their education includes vocational information and training. In many communities, most of the pupils eat the lunch the school serves for them. The effect has been a substantial increase in the total educational task of the school, both in the number of functions which are performed and in the amount of time for which responsibility is taken for the children.

The transfer of some of the family's functions to the school has come about as a natural change in American life, and contrary to the vehement protestations of many critics, it has occurred with the full understanding and approval of the public. This transfer has lessened the responsibilities of the family and increased those of the school. It would seem appropriate, in view of these changes, for the family to share with the school the burden of the functions it formerly performed, but this has happened in only a few American communities. Here and there, parents have organized to assist teachers with their many tasks. But this plan is not likely to become common, for it goes against a strong cultural tendency toward job specialization. In too few cases, responsibility has been shared by increasing financial support of the schools to permit the employment of more adults. As a result, the schools are now in the difficult position of having responsibilities formerly borne by the family, in which they are expected to operate on higher levels of efficiency than most families ever did, yet without corresponding increases in support.

UNDERSTANDING UNNECESSARY TALKING

Talking without permission is one of the most common breaches of discipline. Perhaps this is because it is a rather mild violation of the rules, and so does not ordinarily involve the risk of serious punishment. But this can never be more than a partial explanation. It is even more likely that talking is so common because it expresses children's efforts to satisfy universal human needs for recognition and belonging.

In the folklore of discipline by punishment, unnecessary talking is to be stopped, by force if no other methods are successful. In the science of education, the same unnecessary talking is a problem of behavior which needs to be studied. As a general rule, teachers incline more towards the application of science than the use of folklore, but in some few cases an exasperated teacher may forget about diagnoses. In folklore too much and too loud talking identifies the "fresh kid" who needs to be put in his proper place. Sarcasm is one way to do this: "If I could buy you for what you're worth, and sell you for what you think you're worth, I'd make enough money to retire from teaching." This is intended to be a squelch, and in some cases it works. However, it exhibits an almost complete misunderstanding of the reasons for the "fresh kid's" talking. He more likely wants to bolster his ideas of his own worth than to display them.

Rather, the teacher should try to understand *why* the student talks too much and too loudly. He might find that the "fresh kid" strongly desires recognition, someone to like him, to listen to him, and to need him. These are very common causes of loudness among teenagers who have not learned better ways of gaining attention. Alert teachers know many ways of giving students opportunities to earn recognition—a special report to the class, the writing of directions for sighting in a rifle, or, possibly, participation in the student court. This method of handling insecure talkers enables the teacher to get at the root of the objectionable behavior. It may even convert the problem talker into an asset to the class.

DISCIPLINE THROUGH INTEREST

On one occasion a junior English class in the senior high school beset the teacher with daily behavior problems. All of the incidents were minor, but the total effect was serious enough to interfere with the progress of the class. Assignments to write themes were either disregarded or poorly done. It was evident that the youngsters had no interest in the topics which were assigned to them. However, they were full of complaints about the operation of the school. Perhaps better order could have been maintained by extreme sternness, but order was not regarded as the primary objective of this English class. The principal objective was to improve the students' writing abilities, and this called for measures other than punishment.

Conferences between the teacher and the high-school principal resulted in a plan to appeal to the students' interests. The students were asked to think about their experiences in the high school and to use them as the subjects for short compositions. The best would be published as editorials in the school newspaper. Interest did develop, and class behavior improved. It was no longer a problem. Several of the short themes were printed as editorials, as had been promised.

The point of this incident should be clear. Frustration at uninteresting assignments was eliminated by the substitution of interesting ones. Opportunities for recognition by the entire school were provided by publication of the better themes as editorials. When it became possible for the students to satisfy in desirable activities their natural, personal needs for expression, the need to indulge in undesirable behavior disappeared.

DISCIPLINE THROUGH RECOGNITION

Not all recognition of students by teachers is as elaborate as the incident in the preceding section. An alert teacher knows which children in her class need recognition and tries to satisfy their needs during daily classroom work. Only a skilled observer can be aware of the teacher's intention. For example, a homemaking class in the junior high school is having a discussion about the morning's breakfast. The girls have been asked to read the textbook material on breakfasts, and they have been shown a film strip on the subject. Now the teacher has asked them to tell what they usually eat for their breakfasts. After several have answered, the teacher notices that Edna is shifting about in her seat. She knows that Edna cannot sit for very long without moving or talking, and it has been a few minutes since she has had an opportunity to do either. Now she is ready to do something! How shall the teacher handle Edna's behavior in this situation?

Suppose the teacher should disregard her knowledge of Edna as an individual and let the others continue to report on their breakfast menus. Before long, after one of the girls has said that she had fruit juice, poached eggs on toast, and milk for her breakfast, Edna will erupt with, "I don't never drink milk for breakfast, ha, ha, ha," or something equally inappropriate. The other girls will laugh at the remark, and the teacher will be obliged to scold her for talking without permission. Edna, however, will have had some recognition, and she will now be able to sit quietly for a few more minutes. But how satisfactory are the ways she is learning to get attention? Surely this is not a step toward responsible, adult behavior in a group situation.

Would it not be better for Edna to learn a more acceptable manner of relieving her restlessness? The teacher can contrive some means of giving her an opportunity. After Dorothy has reported a breakfast of fruit, cereal, toast, and milk, the teacher turns to Edna and says, "That's surely a well-balanced breakfast, isn't it, Edna?" Edna smiles. Her reply may be no more than the single word, "Yes." Her need for attention has been met, she and the others have heard the sweet sound of her own name spoken in pleasant tones; she belongs to the class; the other girl feels complimented; and the atmosphere of the class remains serene. Without her knowing it, Edna's responses were shaped into socially approved patterns of behavior. A skillful teacher does this sort of thing many times in the course of a day. It far outdoes the "toughness" so often recommended by folklore.

THE INCIDENT AND THE PROCESS

The folklore of education focuses on conflict, but usually with little regard for the larger situation in which the conflict occurs. An isolated fragment of unsocial behavior presents a challenge to the teacher, whose success is judged by another fragment of behavior, the response that is made to the challenge. Little or no attention is paid to the sequences of interaction which both precede and follow the dramatic incident. Some of the interactions are between teacher and students, others among students alone, and still others between students and persons outside the school. One can hardly understand any incident of behavior without knowing something of the processes of which it is a result, yet in the folk report the incident usually stands alone.

From this folklorist viewpoint, the good teacher is the one who can quell a disturbance. The image of such an authoritarian figure persists in the minds of many adults who remember him or her as the teacher who would not tolerate misconduct. The teacher's actions on the occasions when students violated the school's regulations are remembered. Every teacher who has talked to any extent with parents has heard many descriptions of such incidents.

The unfortunate aspect of this concept is that it considers the incident alone, neglecting the developmental growth of a child, both in and out of the school. At times, a single act of misbehavior may quite properly be treated as an isolated occurrence, but on other occasions some examination of the larger situation will be necessary. No one can be sure just how to characterize any infraction of rules without at least a brief inquiry into the reasons for it.

NECESSARY MISBEHAVIOR

Much student misconduct is necessary in the sense that it is done to satisfy desires for the approval of other persons. When a boy seeks to earn approval by working ten problems quickly and accurately, it is the teacher's esteem he seeks, and the behavior is welcomed. But another boy may win the approval of his teen-age companions by drawing a caricature of the teacher on the chalkboard. It is possible that the boy's status in his own gang will rise as he incurs the displeasure of the teacher. In this respect he may even be said to seek the punishment that will strengthen his position in the gang as it also strengthens the gang's influence with its members. Where this happens, punishment is likely to cause more of the same type of behavior, for others may also need to gain the approval of the gang.

Ideally, a class should consist of students who share the same aims, so that anyone who is punished by the teacher also loses the approval of his classmates. Yet this is seldom the actual situation. More often, at least two different sets of aims compete in the same class. Students guided by one kind of aims seek the teacher's approval; with them even mild punishment is very effective, although it is rarely needed. Their acceptance of the teacher's purposes usually prevents misbehavior. But youngsters motivated by a contrary set of aims may court punishment repeatedly.

Now and then a child's misbehavior cannot be fitted into any preconceived pattern of student misconduct. The student who seeks to please the teacher is easily understood, and the youth who welcomes disapproval is only a little more difficult to comprehend. But how shall we judge the offense when the model student draws the caricature of the teacher? What has made this incongruous piece of behavior necessary for him? It is proper to judge the incident only after careful investigation of all the processes that led to it.

THE DISCIPLINE OF STUDYING A SUBJECT

Another folklorist belief in education regards discipline as resulting from the study of certain subjects. Mathematics, for example, is thought of as disciplining the power of reason, and science is felt to be an excel-

lent training for the power of observation. Though this
view has generally been discredited, it is still current
enough to require consideration at least briefly. The
underlying assumption of this idea is simply that habits
and attitudes that are learned in one situation will
automatically be displayed in other situations as well.
If this were actually true, of course, the task of public
education would be much less difficult than teachers
find it to be. The fact is, however, that people express
different sets of habits and attitudes as they move from
one situation to another. What is learned in one context can be relied on to be operative only in identical
or similar contexts. Change the situation, and you
change the response.

But the study of academic subjects does have important disciplinary effects of another, if more restricted
sort. For in order to make progress in a field of study,
one must obviously apply oneself to learning the particular discipline that is used in that subject. One cannot
get very far in mathematics, for example, unless one
knows and complies with the rules of mathematics, that
is, unless one learns to "think like a mathematician."
And in this sense every academic field of learning is a
discipline. Its learning and effect begin when the study
of a particular subject is first undertaken, usually in
grade school, and continue cumulatively as long as its
study is kept up.

To be sure, the extent to which fields of study require
and impart their own brand of intellectual discipline
varies widely from subject to subject. Sequence in the
organization of materials is of greater importance in
some of the subjects than in others. In mathematics,
science, and foreign languages, for example, the pro-
gression from simple to complex is so important that a

youngster can hardly be intelligent in them unless he has followed the sequence in detail. In other subjects, as for example English and the social studies, the sequence is of less importance until advanced stages of study have been reached.

The discipline exerted by an academic subject is more or less unique in that it is not exactly duplicated in any other. Someone who has learned to think in mathematics will need to learn other ways of thinking for the study of history and shorthand. Every new subject presents the student with the need for a new kind of thinking. The greater the difference between the new subject and those in which the student has already made some progress, the greater the task of learning the new way of thinking will be.

Students who learn to think in the manner required by a particular subject usually do as well in it as their ability permits. Those who do not learn the new mode of thought are often confused and uncertain. The former can recognize in the arithmetic assignments problems which they know how to solve, while the latter see in the same assignments only puzzles which they do not know how to approach. One who knows how to work a problem usually has confidence in his answer, but those to whom the problem is a puzzle are certain neither of the methods they use nor of their answers. These are the students who say, "I just can't do arithmetic." Often their parents concur: "Joan never could do arithmetic." With other students the "can't do" statements may be made in regard to history or foreign language or science.

The folklore of education can neither recognize nor explain what happens to children when they are confronted with the disciplinary requirements of a given subject. Yet it is an exceedingly important aspect of education in times when most youngsters are expected to complete high school. The average length of an adult's formal education has been increasing in this country for many decades. Present indications are that the increase will continue. And the longer the period of formal education in the life of the individual, the more necessary it will be that he accept the disciplines he studies. Otherwise, the value of his education will decrease year by year as its level of advancement increases.

Children's failure to accept discipline in its meaning of learning new kinds of thinking leads to breaches of the discipline which is defined in terms of conduct. Frustration in the puzzle situations results in actions which violate regulations. For as has already been pointed out above, children seldom misbehave when they are able to understand their assignments and have the abilities to do them.

Most responsibility for discipline in the schools is placed upon the teacher. Yet he is also the subject of some of the most preposterous notions in the folklore of education. The next chapter examines some of these folklorist beliefs about teachers and contrasts them with what we know about the real persons who actually teach in our contemporary American schools.

5. Imaginary Teachers Everyone Knows

Teaching is a unique profession. Unlike the people in most other occupations, the teacher spends his working day not with adults but with children. Nor does he have many daytime occasions for contacts with grown-ups in other vocations. Indeed, even teachers in the same school work together only infrequently. And those who teach in different schools have even fewer opportunities for regular contact. It is true, of course, that teachers in the various school subjects can hold sectional meetings once a year at the annual teachers' convention. Yet the most they can accomplish there is to talk about their work. Probably no two of them have ever taught together in one classroom.

Because of this unique aspect of the teaching profession, teachers tend to be separated from the main currents of adult life. They have fewer contacts with people in other occupations; and, what is even more important, the citizens as a whole have fewer contacts with them. Most people, that is to say, must talk *about* teachers a good deal more than they can talk *with* them.

And, as a result, stereotyped images of teachers are able to flourish largely unchecked by knowledge of what teachers and teaching are actually like.

The school administrator, whether superintendent of the city system or principal of one of the buildings, has many more opportunities than the classroom teacher for meeting other adults in the course of his work. He handles most of the school's business transactions, and so becomes acquainted with the merchants and civic leaders of the community. Usually he is a member of one of the local service clubs. Often he is known as a "good fellow" among other adults. Because of his many face-to-face acquaintances, he is not surrounded by as many folklore beliefs as the teacher.

Folk beliefs about teachers are numerous in our society. One of the most interesting is the popular notion that teachers are different from other people. Another is the image of the instructor as the stern taskmaster who makes his pupils "toe the mark." Sometimes the teacher is thought of as a dedicated soul who teaches for the love of it, finding satisfactions more important than salary. In rural areas the position is still regarded as one in which frequent changes are necessary for the good of the school district. By tradition, teachers are expected to begin their careers in small schools from which they may eventually aspire to move to positions in larger cities. As a rule, too, elementary teachers are felt to need less education than those who teach in high school—on the related folklorist assumption that there is such a thing as having too much education to teach in the lower grades. And everywhere today it has become convenient to think of the teacher as a mass baby-sitter upon whom can be loaded more and more of what once were purely the responsibilities of parents.

Perhaps there have been teachers who could actually be fitted into one or another of these popular images. But such stereotypes certainly cannot explain or do justice to teachers and teaching as they really are. For one thing, they grossly oversimplify the nature of the people who teach. And secondly, they are wholly inaccurate.

THE TEACHER WHO IS DIFFERENT FROM OTHER PEOPLE

A common belief today is that teachers can be easily distinguished from other people. Those who express this belief, who can "always tell a teacher," are thereby accomplishing two purposes: they are showing their uninformed listeners how perspicacious they are; and they are indicating their contempt—for the statement that all teachers are alike in being different, is seldom intended as a compliment.

Teachers *are* different, of course. But they are infinitely more different from one another individually than from the general public as a whole. Naturally, anyone can tell a teacher at the annual teachers' convention when all of them are wearing large, distinctive badges. But when the badges come off, it is a different story. Like people in general, teachers come in all sizes, shapes, and ages, pursue all manner of interests and avocations, and exhibit the widest range of personality types and behavior.

At the present time, economic circumstances compel a great many teachers to supplement their meager professional incomes through part-time employment outside the educational system. Yet who would claim to be able to identify the pedagogue in these after-hours situations—as a clerk, a filling station attendant, a truck driver, a bartender, or perhaps the member of a jazz combo? Clearly, the alleged differentness of teachers is nothing more than what might be called identification by association. Once he has left his professional context —the school—the teacher turns out to look and act like anyone else. He is just a person.

Even in their classroom mannerisms teachers are not very alike. In fact, they are undoubtedly as different from one another as are the members of any other profession. Moreover, in view of the backgrounds from which they have entered the teaching profession, this is not at all surprising.

A considerable amount of information has been collected on the kinds of people who become teachers. Like most other persons, they have chosen an occupation which they believe will improve their social and economic status. This means that their families probably were at the social and economic level of the lower middle in their communities. In industrial areas a high percentage of teachers' parents are skilled or semi-skilled workers. In the rural states, the most common parental occupation is farming. Nowhere in the country do many bankers' and executives' sons enter the teaching profession, although a few of their daughters are attracted to it. At the present time, a great many of the men, and some of the women who teach are veterans of military service. Since this is also true of other adults in the same age bracket, it is not a source of observable differences.

Incidentally, the fact that young people seek occupations which will improve personal and family status is one clue to the present shortage of teachers. The profession no longer represents a step up the occupational ladder for as many people as it once did. Instead, it is more likely to be a step down. Hence, teaching cannot attract as many capable young people as it did in other years.

Probably the only real difference between teachers and other persons is the average number of years of school they have completed. In this respect teachers *are* different. The majority of the adult population has not finished high school, but no one can receive a teaching certificate in any state without at least a few credit hours of college work. In most of the states elementary teaching requires several years of college preparation, and the bachelor's degree is needed for high-school teaching. A great many teachers have also received the master's degree for an additional year of college or university study. It should be noted that this difference in number of years of school completed does separate teachers from other adults in the general population— though the difference vanishes when the education of teachers is compared with that of members of the other professions.

In these times, when it is expected that everyone will finish high school, and when the percentages of youth attending and completing college are increasing rapidly, differences in average number of years of education between teachers and other adults may be expected to diminish. The level of education among the entire population has been rising steadily, and the upward trend seems to be growing stronger. In another generation or so, much of the difference in education which now distinguishes the teacher should disappear.

THE STERN TASKMASTER

The folk belief in the stern taskmaster who is said to inhabit so many classrooms probably owes its survival to the comfort parents obtain from it, for doubtless it is reassuring to feel that *someone* is firm with one's children. So the image persists of the strict teacher who permits no deviations in pupil behavior. It is expressed in such pithy statements as, "She makes them work," and, "They can't get away with anything in his classes." These and similar comments are frequent and nearly always uttered in a tone of approval.

Sometimes, of course, the taskmaster viewpoint is intended to express an ideal, rather than to describe an actual teacher. It voices what "ought to be," not "what is." Most often, it occurs among parents who have had difficulty in controlling their own children. Apparently they expect the school to exhibit more firmness than the home. They expect the teacher to instruct their children in manners, to compel them to do their homework, and to build up their character and morals. What they are thereby expressing is the old, familiar fantasy of the fixed standard and the uniform student.

The image of the taskmaster dwells in the memories of the many people who can now recall similar characteristics of instructors that they once had. Teachers hear many reminiscences of this sort in their conversations with parents: the class of long ago in which no one dared to whisper; the principal who stood in the corridor where he pounced upon any student who broke a rule. Very likely these legendary persons are admired more now than they were at the time, but the clear implication is that today's teachers should be more like the memory of teachers in the Good Old Days.

One of the fallacies of this viewpoint is that it imputes to teachers qualities of omnipotence which they do not have, any more than other people do. Only from a considerable distance is it possible to believe that one person can know and control every aspect of the behavior of thirty or thirty-five other persons. Perhaps it is the long span of intervening years that obscures such obvious realities. Or it may be the fact that so few people are familiar enough with the teacher's actual job. At any rate, closer attention to the educational facts of life would reveal only too clearly that the image of the teacher as taskmaster is a most misleading over-simplification.

A classroom is a social situation involving innumerable relationships in an ever changing context. Relationships between teacher and pupils, and among pupils, are constantly being formed and modified in the series of events which occur there. These relationships are also changed by experiences which teachers and children have outside the classroom. While the teacher may at times be a taskmaster, he may also be called upon to play several other important roles, among them those of friend, confidant, sympathizer, guide, and partner in work. Moreover, the combinations of his roles are not exactly the same for any two pupils, nor do they remain the same for one child over an extended period of time. Not only must the teacher be able to play all of these roles, but he also needs the ability to create them for himself in individual and group situations.

The view of the teacher as taskmaster is far too narrow to encompass such broad social functions. If it could somehow become an accurate description, the scope of instruction would be limited to a unilateral teacher-pupil relationship in which all of the direction of the pupils' activities originated with the teacher. The notion seems to envision a classroom in which every child's attention is focused always and exclusively upon the teacher, with all activities awaiting the latter's signals. This is sheer myth, for in America at least, no such classroom ever existed.

The most serious criticism that can be made of the taskmaster image is that it fails to place a fair share of the responsibility for learning upon the child. Youngsters are growing up in many ways during their years in the school. Among other things, they are learning to bear responsibility for their actions. This sort of maturing cannot happen unless children have opportunities to do some things on their own. This is impossible when an adult makes all of their decisions. The taskmaster who permits his students no scope to plan, to work, and to make mistakes, limits their opportunities for learning to assume responsibility.

The notion of the taskmaster errs also in the expectation of uniformity in the behavior of teachers and children. This is only a slight variation of the myth of the uniform child which was examined in Chapter III. Instead of regarding all children as alike, it considers that the teacher must make them behave alike. Even if this were possible, it would be a most unfortunate form of education, for in order to realize their individual potentialities, children need to learn to be different.

THE DEDICATED TEACHER

It has long been held that teaching is one of the most highly satisfying occupations. Numerous persons have grouped the profession with medicine and the ministry as the three vocations which afford the greatest opportunities to serve mankind. Emphasis upon the satisfactions to be obtained from service is used to recruit young people for teaching, as well as in the reminiscences of those who are near the close of their professional careers.

It is true that there are intangible rewards for the teacher who guides a student through the solution of a difficult personal problem. The satisfactions of the pupil are shared as success and accomplishment emerge from threatened failure. Every teacher experiences and values these warm feelings of gratification. But they are not enjoyed as often as could be desired.

The teacher must also share in a great many failures and disappointments. The satisfaction of success in arousing a truant's interest in school is likely to be experienced less frequently than the frustration of watching a student drop out of school. Most trying of all are the youngsters teetering on the edge of delinquency. Since the problems in such cases are usually complex and deep-rooted, all of a teacher's efforts may come to naught. Teaching must therefore be recognized as a profession involving a great deal of frustration as well as satisfaction.

The belief that any substantial number of people are attracted into teaching because of its opportunities for service can only be regarded as an anachronism in the highly intensified money economy in which we live today. Money "talks" more loudly these days than ever before. The image of the dedicated person who teaches for the love of it is not vocationally attractive to very many young persons in our society. Anyone who attempts to enlist American youth in the middle of the twentieth century into any financially unrewarded service goes against some very strong economic currents. The facts are that students of high academic ability are not being attracted into teaching at the present time in numbers adequate to maintain the profession, and these facts have been widely publicized by every possible medium. It should be evident that the folk beliefs in the satisfactions of teaching have little influence in such important decisions as the choice of careers. The economic and prestige rewards for teaching must be raised substantially if enough teachers of high quality are to be found to staff the public schools.

Community treatment of the teacher has been slow to change to conform with practices in business and industry. The principle of a definite number of hours in the work week, with overtime pay for extra hours, is firmly established in most sections of the American economy. Yet it is still part of the folklore of American education that the teacher should perform many extra duties without extra compensation. Evening and weekend hours of planning and marking papers are considered to be part of the job. If the school board is generous, the teacher may receive an extra payment of $75 for the year-long responsibility of serving as adviser for the high-school yearbook. Not $75 per week, of course, nor even $75 per month, but $75 for the entire year.

Teaching has not even been able to hold all of the persons who entered the profession in its better years. Thousands upon thousands have left for other occupations. Many teachers have found it a perplexing and painful decision to leave the vocation for which their college years prepared them and in which their adult lives have been spent. But surely no one can question their right to change to any position which promises greater individual rewards.

The free choice of occupations has been one of the great instruments of social mobility in American society. For generations people have attempted to improve their personal and family stations by selecting vocations which offered the rewards they sought. Teachers also cherish ambitions to get ahead. It is discomforting for them to see so many unskilled occupations with low educational requirements rewarded more generously than their own demanding work. Their remuneration hardly compares with conditions in the other professions. For instance, the value of the orthodontia in a single classroom is often greater than the teacher's annual salary.

A certain amount of occupational shifting is normal among adults, for it is to be expected that some persons will find other vocations more attractive than those they first entered. In the long run, however, the numbers entering and leaving any stable occupation should be approximately the same. There can be no doubt about the continuing need for teachers; no abrupt decreases in the number of teaching positions have occurred, nor do any appear likely in the future. Indeed, the trend in the number of positions is slightly upward. Yet the fact remains that for teaching, recent occupational shifts have been a one-way traffic out of the profession.

It is very probable that the concept of the dedicated teacher is in large measure simply a rationalization of our society's unwillingness to reward teachers adequately for their work. It is not a view that teachers themselves express very often, and when they do, it is more apt to be in a mood of retrospection than anticipation. The personal satisfactions of teaching are no more than one of numerous incentives for entering the profession. Rarely would they be sufficient inducement to influence the choice of a permanent career.

The American people have been thoroughly convinced of the personal economic advantages of education. Undoubtedly one of the principal reasons for their support of the public schools has been the desire to provide opportunities for their children to share in these advantages. Yet they ignore similar aspirations of the persons who teach, and the economic incentives for teaching have fallen below those of many less demanding occupations. Preparation for a career in teaching is no longer a sound investment, for teaching today can offer no more financial rewards for a college education than energetic youth can realize without it.

THE ITINERANT PEDAGOGUE

"I guess we'll have to let Miss Lucy go this spring." One of the trustees of the one-room country school was speaking of their teacher.

"Isn't she a good teacher?"

"Oh, yes! She's the best teacher we ever had. But this is her third year here, and we think that's long enough. It's time for her to find another school."

This trustee's attitude was very common in the past among the patrons of the public schools. Now, in the urban centers it seldom confronts teachers any more, but in the rural areas of the country, people still believe in the benefits of itinerancy.

The teacher cast in the role of an itinerant journeyman, unlike the three fictitious images previously discussed, is an unfortunate reality to many thousands of public school teachers. Their nomadic situations are not imaginary. The notion that their forced itinerancy is beneficial is an expensive illusion. Frequent changes from school to school are costly not only for the teacher but for the community as well, since the quality of education is inevitably lowered.

The concept of the itinerant pedagogue flourishes where teaching is not regarded as a profession. In the city school systems, the employment of teachers has become a specialized function performed by professional school administrators. The superintendent of schools exercises this function, or delegates it to his administrative assistants. School-board approval of the administration's personnel recommendations is almost universally routine. The permanence which is accorded teachers' positions in such systems enables them to become more and more proficient in their tasks. These veteran teachers are the greatest assets of the city school systems.

The usual practices of employing teachers are quite different in most small school systems. Here, the members of the board of education delegate fewer decisions to the superintendent, and they participate much more directly in the administration of the school, including the hiring of teachers. In the smallest schools, the rural, one-room elementary schools, there are neither principals nor superintendents. The trustees are the administration—and the teachers' tenure is at its shortest.

Annual rates of personnel turnover in large city schools are minimal compared with the rate of turnover in smaller communities. This has been true for administrators as well as for teachers. Anyone who persists in teaching in rural areas must be prepared for a nomadic life, moving from school to school every two to three years. Occasionally the stay may be longer, but no one can depend upon it, and it may be less. Cases are on record of persons who have been principal in five different village high schools in five consecutive years.

Since recent trends toward the consolidation of districts have reduced the number of small schools, the folk belief in the advantages of moving teachers around now affects fewer people than in the past. However, there are still large numbers of persons who teach in small schools. Moreover, huge areas, particularly in the Great Plains States, are so sparsely populated that even with the consolidation of districts, the schools will continue to be small. For at least another generation, the small school will be characteristic in rural areas of the United States. Unless community attitudes change abruptly, the itinerant pedagogue will also continue to be a widespread phenomenon.

Knowing how uncertain their positions are, the administrators and teachers concerned are obliged to live lives of continuing insecurity. Whatever sustains them must come from outside of their schools and school districts. Every two or three years they must spend considerable time and energy looking for another position and transferring themselves from one community to find roots in another.

At the same time, of course, the educational program runs grave dangers of deteriorating. For with a constant replacement of teachers, there can be no continuity in education either. It is not unusual, for example, for some village schools to have no one on the faculty who has taught there for longer than two years. Occasionally, the entire staff of five or six teachers leaves at the end of the school year, and a completely new faculty takes over. In effect, this means an annual reorganization, a beginning of the schools' operations all over again.

Such inefficiencies of the small rural school are in the first instance the affair of those living in the communities concerned. Yet in a larger sense, they are everyone's business. For since it is the cities that attract the country-side's surplus labor, the effects of lower quality education are soon felt by everyone. Greater professionalization of rural school teachers will benefit the entire nation.

In times when teachers are in plentiful supply, the administrators of city school systems seldom welcome inexperienced teachers to employment. Many an aspiring college graduate has been told by a friendly superintendent, "Get yourself a year or two of experience, and we'll be glad to have your application." Naturally, such policies are subject to variations in the supply of employable teachers. In the depression years of the Thirties, when many people sought employment as teachers, even small schools with no more than a dozen teachers could announce that only experienced teachers would be considered for vacancies. But with the well-publicized teacher shortage of the Fifties, many city school systems have quite willingly employed inexperienced persons.

Large schools have good reasons to be confident that they can attract experienced teachers from the smaller schools, for they can offer many professional advantages: a higher salary, an automatic schedule of salary increments, more liberal sick leave provisions, superior equipment, more opportunity to specialize, and greater personal privacy. Heavier teaching loads of larger classes are often balanced by lighter responsibility for extracurricular activities, which in the small school may amount to several activities for each teacher. These advantages are attractive enough to entice a fair number of superintendents and principals of village schools to seek classroom teaching positions in city systems. The faculty of nearly every large school includes a few former administrators.

Belief in the necessity of the village apprenticeship is tinged with the inconsistency of folklore. Policies of employing only experienced teachers imply that small schools are inferior to large schools, for in effect the latter are saying, "Teachers good enough for your students are not good enough for ours." If there *were* any relationship between ability and reward in teaching, there would be much truth in such a comparison, for the rewards are undeniably greater in the larger school systems. But, such a relationship has never been demonstrated; good teachers are found in schools of all sizes.

Policies which exclude the inexperienced from employment also imply that teaching in the small school is an apprenticeship for a position in a large school. Presumably, the beginning teacher is to spend a period of several years as half-apprentice and half-journeyman before achieving the eminence of master teacher in the city school. The professional path from small school to large has been traveled by large numbers of teachers.

Something of a paradox is discernible in the two implications discussed above. If the small schools were really inferior, experience gained in them would hardly be the best preparation for teaching in the larger and better schools. It might even be proposed that teachers should go first to the large school where their introductory and most formative experiences could be provided under the best circumstances possible. But apart from considerations of quality, teaching in small and large schools is sufficiently different that neither prepares very well for the other. A better and more realistic plan would be for the beginning teacher to apprentice in the same sort of school as that in which his permanent teaching is expected to be done.

THE BABY-SITTER

In the minds of many parents the school has acquired a new function of taking the children off the family's hands for as much time as possible. This is an aspect of the folklore of education which is still in the growing stage. It may be that in time it will come to be regarded as the most important function of the public school. It makes of the teacher a mass baby-sitter who frees the home of daytime responsibility for the children.

Years ago, when the work of the children was needed at home, parents often begrudged the time spent in school. But children's help is seldom needed in the modern home, and when it is sought, it is likely to be in experiences contrived for their beneficial effects upon the children's growth rather than for the actual value of their work. Only a small percentage of American families today have any real need for their children's help, but a very large number of families badly need to find wholesome things for their children to do. Cities especially have a dearth of open fields and woods, skating ponds, and "ole swimmin' holes." Even the low-income families, which are larger in number than most middle-class persons imagine, have little need of the help of their small children. It will be different when they are old enough to bring in extra income.

For the mother of several small children, a rainy day in summer can be a minor catastrophe. The chore of finding something for the children to do lets up for her only at bedtime. Most trying of all in this regard is the late summer, after the vacation camps and recreational centers have closed and before classes begin on Labor Day. By this time everyone in the family is longing for the reopening of school.

It is the usual policy in school administration to set a date by which a child must reach his sixth birthday in order to enter the first grade at the opening of school in September. In cities with a preliminary year of kindergarten, the date is established for the fifth birthday. Sometimes the date is set by state law instead of in the local school system. It may be the first day of October, or the last day of December, or any other agreed time in autumn or early winter. Whatever the date, and whoever sets it, inevitably the birthdays of some children just miss it. Their parents are thereby compelled to keep them at home for another year. One may contemplate such prospects light-heartedly when others are affected by them; but they are serious matters to the parents concerned—and these can also make them a considerable headache for superintendents of schools and elementary principals.

Now and then, when the crucial date has been locally established, a superintendent makes the mistake of changing it by a few days, perhaps from the first to the fifteenth of October. The inducement to change is that it will please the parents of children whose birthdays happen to fall within the added period. But on the average the change is likely to arouse an equal number of parents who will agitate for the date to be moved back to the first of November, their case made stronger by the precedent of the first change. The superintendent soon realizes that he has made a mistake. He can expect a good deal of emotion to be directed at him, and he may find himself defending the entire policy of admission to the first year of school before a mass meeting of mothers.

People who highly value the baby-sitting aspect of education must realize that its price may be an increasing neglect of other educational functions. Indeed, should the task of keeping children away from their homes gain precedence over their instruction, the day may come when the excellence of a school is measured by the number of hours per day and days per year it is in session! This would amount to a drastic reversal of the standards by which schools have up to now been judged. Of course, the new criterion would be easy to apply, for the best school would simply be the one that keeps the children longest. Possibly, even, children might learn more in the lengthened hours. But this could certainly not be guaranteed, since the reason for the expanded time spent in schools would have little to do with the purposes of education as traditionally understood.

THE ELEMENTARY TEACHER WHO NEEDS LESS EDUCATION

The widespread belief that elementary-school teachers need less education than high-school teachers probably originated in the differences in the difficulty of the subjects which are taught in these two levels of public education. For example, algebra and geometry are more advanced than arithmetic; *A Tale of Two Cities* is more complex than *Black Beauty*. Since the elementary subjects are simpler than those in the secondary school, it is presumed to follow that less education is needed to teach them. The viewpoint is sometimes carried to the extreme that it is possible to have too much education to teach in the elementary school.

The supposed difference in the amount of education needed is only one of several factors in the public's view of elementary and high-school teaching. The teaching of most high-school subjects (homemaking and girls' physical education are the obvious exceptions) is much more likely to be a masculine occupation than the teaching of any elementary grade. Rewards of prestige and salary have usually been greater in the high school, although the financial differences are disappearing as the single salary schedule becomes universal.

It is worth noting at this point that elementary and secondary teaching are only two levels in an extensive hierarchy of teaching positions. The relative status of teaching was expressed conversationally by the dean of a university college of education in words approximately as follows:

"I climbed the ladder myself. I began teaching in a one-room country school. My next job was in a village elementary school. Then I taught in a town high school. After that I was a superintendent in a small town. From there I moved to college teaching, and then to teaching graduate courses. Now I am a dean."

In many school systems a transfer from the elementary to the high school is regarded as a promotion. Sometimes it is conferred as a reward to an elementary teacher who has pleased the administration, while a transfer in the opposite direction has been used to discipline an unruly personality in the high school. In either case, the transfer is no more than an administrative exploitation of the general attitude toward elementary and high-school positions.

The facts are, of course, that the average elementary

teacher has had fewer years of college education than the average secondary teacher. A good many of the former have taken less than four years of college, while very nearly all high-school teachers have at least bachelor's degrees, signifying the completion of four years of college or university work. A number of states now issue elementary teaching certificates upon the completion of a college curriculum of one, two, or three years. In some few cases, people who have had no education beyond the high school are teaching in rural elementary schools. The cities have generally had much more success than the towns and villages in employing four-year elementary teachers. The average elementary teachers' education varies directly with the size of the communities in which they teach, but the number of years of college for high-school teachers is nearly the same everywhere.

These differences in teacher education are the results of tradition and expediency, not of any generally accepted professional educational aims. The tradition in question dates back more than half a century to the time when normal schools, dispensing secondary rather than college level education, turned out most of the elementary school teachers. These normal schools many years ago gave way to four-year teachers' colleges. Yet their influence still survives in the low esteem in which many people continue to hold elementary teacher education. More recently, moreover, this negative attitude was temporarily reinforced because of the large-scale hiring of less than fully qualified teachers during the teacher shortage following upon World War II. Since the advent of the four-year teachers' colleges, however —and aside from special emergency measures—professional teacher education does not recognize any differences, either in quality or quantity, between elementary and secondary preparation for teaching. The two preparations differ greatly in the types of courses taken because of the differences in the work to which they lead. Yet as far as length and quality are concerned, the two programs are intended to be equal.

Probably no one engaged in teacher education regards the elementary curricula of less than four full years of college as anything more than temporary attempts to alleviate the postwar shortage. In this respect, these curricula are in the same category as the emergency certification of unqualified teachers. Virtually everyone would like to discontinue both practices as soon as possible, for they can only be regarded as unfortunate expediencies which run counter to the long-term trend toward a four-year college minimum for the elementary teacher.

The real differences in elementary and secondary teacher education parallel organizational differences in the two schools. The secondary teacher is a specialist in a departmentalized institution. Under favorable conditions all of his teaching is done in a single subject field, although his education usually includes specialization in at least two high-school subjects. In contrast, the typical elementary teacher is a generalist who must be able to teach all of the common subjects. Here the specialization is in the grade instead of the subject.

Although it is natural for any teacher to consider his own assignment as the most complex of all, the art of teaching is substantially the same at all grade levels. Because whatever is taught must be taught to human beings, the same professional skills and understandings are essential everywhere, and the need for teachers with culture and intelligence is universal.

Undoubtedly, a considerable amount of self-interest has kept alive the folk belief that some teachers need less education than others. It is a convenient argument for employing less capable teachers at lower salaries, and thereby apparently reducing the cost of public education. Yet those who argue in this manner do not expect to economize by using the services of less capable doctors and nurses when the small children are to be treated than when the teen-agers and adults are ill.

Differences in the education of teachers are only one of many factors which eventually appear as larger or smaller items in the school budget. The expenses of operating the public schools must be considered in connection with virtually every problem in education. Here too, folklore and custom have developed to confuse public understanding of the financing of the public schools. The next chapter presents an analysis of some of the folk beliefs in this area in the light of what is known to be needed.

6. The Anachronisms of Financing Public Education

The operation of the public schools is a heavy financial burden for most American communities. Educational costs often amount to half or even more of our cities' expenditures. Schools are expensive, and the expense has increased greatly in the last fifteen years in at least three respects. In the first place, along with nearly everything else upon which prices can be set, school costs have gone up rapidly since World War II. It costs much more to provide in 1960-61 the same education that was offered in 1944-45. Secondly, the tendency to expect more services from the public schools has added some new costs to the increases in the older expenses. Parents have not been satisfied for their children to have in 1960-61 the same education other children received in 1944-45. Every new service which has been added for today's children has enlarged the school budget to some extent. Increases in costs have accompanied such new arrangements as bus transportation to and from the school, special education for handicapped children, and programs of guidance and remedial reading.

These items present serious problems in school financing. To them must be added a third type of expenditure for the construction of new school buildings. The Fifties have been a period of universal overcrowding of the schools. Millions of children from the high-birth-rate years immediately following World War II entered the schools, and millions more were soon to follow. Nationally, school facilities are now needed for some four million children to enter each year in contrast to slightly over two million twenty years ago. Yet many communities have been unable to bear the expense of needed additions and replacements for their school plants. Even to provide funds for current operating expenses has been extremely difficult in many cases.

DIFFERENCES IN COMMUNITIES' ABILITIES TO FINANCE SCHOOLS

The greatest single deterrent to adequate financing of public education is the folk practice of depending too heavily upon local sources of revenue. The principle of wholly local support for the public schools is unrealistic in the economic circumstances of American life at the present time. It is also inconsistent with some long-term population trends.

American communities differ greatly both in their financial resources and in the proportions of children in their populations. Often one city has several times as much in property values for each child to be educated as another city. Several factors, either singly or in combination, operate to bring about such different conditions.

The presence of industry adds considerably to the amount of taxable property within a city's boundaries. Since some communities have many industries, and oth-

ers have few or none, this is a common source of differences in local tax-raising abilities. The school district
in which little or no industrial property is located is at
a serious disadvantage, for its residential property must
bear a very heavy share of the local tax burden.
Through the cumulative effects of its payrolls, industry
also aids school revenues by raising average family incomes in the community. Although the local authority
cannot tax incomes directly, it does levy upon the additional property values which result from higher incomes. The presence in the community of more property of higher value means more school revenue from
local taxes.

A second factor in local differences in financial ability is the value of the land in the school district. In
rural areas the land surrounding the town may or may
not be included in the school district's taxable resources.
If the district has been consolidated, it will include a
large area of farm or ranch land. And the greater the
dimensions of the district, the greater will be its ability
to raise tax funds for school purposes. Differences in
the quality of the land also affect school revenues, for
fertile acres can contribute more in tax revenue than
poor soil. The products of the rich soil also build a
higher general level of prosperity throughout the area,
and thus again increase the potential income of the
school district. Where no consolidation has been effected, the property within the town or village must
carry the entire burden of local school taxation.

Suburban communities illustrate another kind of local difference in potential school revenue. In one case,
the prestige occupations are heavily represented in an
upper middle-class residential suburb, in which high
family incomes and home values compensate for lack

of industry. The public schools in such a community can be maintained on adequate financial levels without undue strain. In another situation, perhaps only a mile or two away, an expanding "fringe area," which began as a narrow strip of homes and small businesses along a highway entering the larger city, has grown into an independent municipality. Here the business ventures are likely to be precarious, the rates of transiency are high, and both family incomes and home values are low. Only with the greatest difficulty can the schools be financed from local resources. The first of these two common types of communities can support an excellent school system with less effort than the second can provide a meager program of public education.

Financial inequalities among communities are sometimes ameliorated, but often compounded, by differences in the numbers of children to be educated. Where low resources and large numbers of children occur together, the school district is barely able to finance its schools. In contrast, a city with a large total of property value and a relatively small number of children has many times more ability to finance public education. Such differences among cities clearly show the difficulties of using local tax revenues as the sole support of our adequate system of public schools.

THE AMERICAN PEOPLE CAN AFFORD EXCELLENT SCHOOLS

The ability of the American economy to support schools of high quality is beyond question. The total annual cost of maintaining excellent public schools everywhere in this country would require no more than five or six percent of the gross national product, which is approximately the share that Russia is said to apportion to education. This amount would provide an average annual expenditure of about $500 per child if all youngsters entered kindergarten at five and remained in school through the twelfth grade. Such a sum would enable every local district to offer the high quality of education which now is found in only the wealthier districts. At the present time, school expenditures are less than the amounts spent for each one of innumerable luxuries and frivolities. Numerous comparisons have shown that the United States actually spends less on the education of its children than on such items as alcohol, tobacco, or cosmetics. The figure of $500 per child should not be considered excessive for education of high quality. Several entire states now average fairly close to this amount, and many communities exceed it.

Incontrovertible evidence that the American people can afford whatever they desire strongly enough can be seen everywhere. One of the most obvious changes in the appearance of American communities in recent years has been the sprouting of a veritable jungle of television antennas, yet in most cities the purchase of the family's television set has been a larger expenditure than the year's school taxes. Moreover, the nearly universal presence of television in the home has made possible the growth of an entire television industry, of which the expenses are paid indirectly by the public. To take another familiar example, the average annual depreciation on the family car, if it is a recent model, is much more than the taxes paid for educational purposes. While it is true that incomes in a great many households are too low to support such large purchases regularly, they are normal in an enormous number of American families. Private purchases of automobiles have made necessary the construction and renovation of streets, highways and throughways involving public expenditures many times larger than those for education. A billion dollars is big money when it is proposed for federal scholarships, but highway programs are announced for forty or fifty times as much.

The capacity of the economy to expand so as to furnish markets or new products, and even whole new industries, has been demonstrated many times. The radio and television industry, for example, has emerged and developed within the lifetime of a large part of the population, and its market has grown with it. The same is true of the aviation industry, as well as a number of others of recent origin. Beginning about twenty years ago, the entire nation constituted itself a market for arms and munitions on a scale beyond anything anyone had ever envisioned.

Although the temptation to say that the American people value such luxuries as liquor and cosmetics more highly than the quality of their children's education has been irresistible for many persons, expenditures for luxuries and education are so different that the comparison is misleading. People do not "buy" public schools in the same manner as they do lipstick and whiskey. The purchase of merchandise requires only the agreement of a single individual or family, while the approval of expenditures for education is a public decision. And, being a public decision, it is a collective, rather than individual matter and, hence, can be reached only after much longer processes of deliberation. The most energetic merchandising campaign need obtain only a small percentage of sales among its potential customers to be successful, whereas a local proposition for the construction of school buildings fails unless it secures a majority of votes in a community-wide special election. Moreover, though no one circulates petitions against the purchase of beauty aids, a proposal to erect new school buildings is almost certain to be met by vigorous, organized opposition.

None of our luxury expenditures could be said to drain our resources to the point where we cannot *afford* adequate financing of our schools. Meager support of public education is thus not a matter of economic necessity. The nation's wealth remains more than ample to finance the highest-level education that the citizenry may be willing to approve.

EXPORTATION OF EDUCATION

The financing of public education from local resources exclusively, even if it were economically feasible, inflicts an injustice upon the residents of the sparsely populated areas of the United States. Taxpayers in these areas have long been educating many of the future citizens of the larger cities. One of the oldest and most continuous population movements in this country has been the migration of youth from rural to urban areas. Since the first federal census in 1790, the percent of urban population has increased steadily for each ten year period, and the percent of rural population has declined. For all of these generations the farms and villages have exported their youth—along with the education they have paid for—to the cities.

At current costs of public education, a high-school graduate who leaves the village to seek his fortune in the city takes with him at *least* three thousand dollars worth of elementary and secondary education. In some cases he will go to a city within the same state, but often he crosses state lines and so becomes an even greater loss to the community that paid for his education.

CHANGING TAX STRUCTURES

Tax structures have undergone tremendous changes since the days when it was necessary to depend upon local property taxes as the sole support of the public schools. In recent decades, new and highly productive forms of taxation have been developed to increase public revenues. One need mention as examples only the sales tax, which has come into common use among the states, and the federal income tax. But it has not been possible to originate comparable sources of tax revenue which can be used to advantage by local communities. Few cities can make use of either a sales tax or an income tax. They must still rely upon the property tax for the bulk of local revenues, including the funds to be used for education.

The basic facts of tax structures and local resources can only lead to the conclusion that purely local financing of public schools is an anachronism in the contemporary American economy. In a very large number of cases, local taxation can barely raise enough funds to meet the current expenditures for education, leaving nothing for replacing or enlarging present buildings. Yet, an educational burden which is impossible to bear locally becomes much lighter when the more flexible resources of the state can be made available, and still easier when it is regarded as a federal obligation.

STATE FUNDS NOW AID LOCAL DISTRICTS

The need for broader tax bases than the single community has been widely recognized in recent years. Accordingly, most states have developed plans for aiding local districts in the financing of their public schools. Many forms of state aid have been devised to supplement local school funds, both by adding to the general budget and by supplying money for specific purposes such as transportation of students to and from the school and education for handicapped children. The use of the state's superior taxing power has done much to equalize local differences in ability to finance public education. The folk custom of supporting each school district from local resources has been overcome to a considerable extent by programs of state aid for the public schools.

THE NEED FOR FEDERAL FUNDS

Yet there are also great differences among the states. And little has been done to alleviate the effects of such differences upon education. States vary in their abilities to support schools just as their local school districts vary. For one thing, there are great differences in wealth among the states. For another, the number of children to be educated varies. And the rural states still export many of their educated youth. It is only a little more logical to consider the financing of public schools a state responsibility than to regard it as a local obligation. Shifting a substantial part of the financial load to the state improves local conditions, but not as much as is needed, for the shift cannot make up for the inequalities among the states.

The logic of the whole situation points directly to the need for a large scale program of federal aid for public education to help equalize conditions among the states, as state aid has done among local school districts.

The use of federal funds would enable the states to make further equalizations within their boundaries.

Both state and federal programs of financial aid to the public schools involve many technical and administrative considerations which are beyond the scope of the discussion presented here. The formulas for equitable distribution of funds are somewhat complex. However, there is no lack of either study or expertise in this area of school finance. Enough is known to ensure that adequate distribution of funds can be planned and administered.

At the present time a limited amount of federal aid to the public schools is provided, chiefly in the field of vocational education. It comes to local schools through the administration of state boards to aid in financing the teaching of such subjects as agriculture, homemaking, and retailing. The general pattern of federal aid for vocational education began about forty years ago with the original Smith-Hughes Act, and it has been continued and enlarged by subsequent acts of Congress. The most that this plan has contributed to the educational expenses of any state is about 5 percent. Since nearly all of the federal aid to schools has been limited to vocational education, its effect as an equalizing agent among the states has been small. But, at least, it has shown the feasibility of supplementing state resources with federal assistance.

The most recent legislation, the National Defense Educational Act of 1958, follows the earlier patterns in authorizing funds for *specific* purposes, although the scope of the program is undeniably broader than before. Generous aid has been provided for student loans and fellowships. Indeed, the act's provisions clearly reflect the public's views that a crisis in public education is imminent. Financial aid is designated "for strengthening science, mathematics, and modern foreign language instruction," and for "guidance, counseling, and testing." Faith in the power of mechanical teaching aids is evidenced in the authorization of grants for "research and experimentation in more effective utilization of television, radio, motion pictures, and related media for educational purposes." Yet in principle, the act introduced nothing new. The terms of the act continue to prohibit federal control over any educational institution. And its provisions are far from constituting a program for *general* financial aid to education. Moreover, the act grants only a few dollars during its four years of operation for each child who attends the public schools. The annual reimbursement to a school district will be only a fraction of one percent of the local school budget.

But the most serious limitation of the National Defense Education Act is its requirement that local districts match, dollar for dollar, the money which is offered for strengthening their educational programs. Wealthy communities can do this easily, but many of the poorer districts will have great difficulty in finding additional funds for their share of equipment purchases. The act can therefore be considered hardly more than a promising step toward real federal aid to education.

COLLEGES ALSO NEED FEDERAL AID

At the level of higher education, local financing is replaced by state support. Whether it be a state university, a state college, or a teachers' college, an institution of higher learning is considered by a community not as an obligation but as a special resource. Its presence means prestige as well as economic advantages.

Without costing the community a cent in direct outlay, it may be its "leading industry."

Differences in local abilities to finance education do not affect institutions which are supported by state funds, for public colleges and universities are the obligation of the entire state. Local areas of every degree of wealth contribute through various forms of state taxation to the support of the institution, regardless of the numbers of students they may send to it.

Differences in wealth among the states, however, enable some of them to support their public institutions more generously than is possible in other states. Variations in the level of financial support are reflected in every phase of institutional operations. The differences in physical plant may be seen in a casual drive past the campus. Only a little more study is needed to reveal further differences in equipment, library facilities, and faculty salaries. Indeed, differences among states in their ability to support public institutions of higher education are almost as great as the differences among local school districts in their support of their public schools.

Such financial variations inevitably affect the quality of learning experiences for college and university students, just as the same sort of variations affect the learnings of children in the public schools. In terms of opportunities to learn, more funds are the means of expansion and enrichment. Here too, money talks, as it does in most of our culture. More money means better quality faculty, libraries, classrooms, equipment, and laboratories.

All of the arguments in favor of equalizing educational opportunities for children in the public schools seem to apply at the level of public higher education.

From the humanitarian viewpoint, youth of college age surely are as deserving of the best learning opportunities as their younger brothers and sisters. It is hard to find reasons why students in a wealthy state should enjoy richer college experiences than those who happened to be born in a state with fewer resources.

The state invests heavily in the higher education of its youth, and often exports its investment. Rarely will the individual student's payment of tuition and fees amount to more than 25 percent of the total cost of his education in a public institution of higher education in his own state. Often it is much less. There are still state colleges and universities where fees and tuition for a resident of the state amount to as little as one or two hundred dollars per year, which may be only 10 or 20 percent of the total cost of his education. The rest is paid for by the people of the state as an investment in public education. At the very *least,* the public investment in each student who completes a four-year course in a state college will amount to $1,500, and usually it will be much more. In the case of a college graduate who accepts employment in another state, his own state makes an export of this expense in addition to the export of the investment in the graduate's education in the elementary and secondary schools. The total exportation for one graduate's twelve years in the public schools and four years in college may easily exceed $5,000.

The welfare of the nation is as dependent upon the quality of education its young people receive in college as in the elementary and secondary schools, perhaps more so, for the college education makes the public school learnings more useful. The sharing of federal funds to bring conditions among the states nearer to equality of educational opportunity is needed at every level of public education.

FEDERAL RESPONSIBILITY AND LOCAL CONTROL

The principle of local autonomy in public education is of long standing, and it has become firmly established in administrative practice. The United States has never had a national organization of its public schools, and the federal government has never attempted to exercise control over them. Obligation, control, and responsibility have all been located in the states and their communities. Education has been designated as a state function, and this principle has been followed by the organization of state school systems. Within the states both tradition and legislation have delegated the actual administration of the schools to local boards of education. While it has been usual for the states to have retained some degree of regulation and supervision over the schools within their boundaries, the latter have been operated primarily as local school systems.

No doubt one reason for the lack of federal control of the schools has been the absence of federal support. The control of public education has tended to reside in the sources of funds, and these have been almost entirely in the communities and states. Since little federal support has been given to education, occasions for federal regulation have been few. However, in those types of education for which federal funds have been provided, for example, vocational education, controls have accompanied the grants of aid.

Any extension of federal aid to education must, then, bring into consideration the question whether federal controls should also be extended. Both sides of the issue can be supported by strong arguments of precedent. The well-established principle of local autonomy in the administration of the public schools can be presented as the basis for apportioning federal funds to the states without restrictions upon their use. Likewise, a considerable degree of federal control over the state use of funds supplied for education can be argued from the precedents already established in the limited distribution of financial aid for vocational education. This position may be reinforced by the proposition that it is logical to protect any federal investment in education with some control over its expenditure.

The question of federal control over education is more controversial in some respects than in others. Probably no lengthy objections would be raised to federal regulation of minimum standards. Reasonably quick agreement might be expected on specifications for equipment and supplies, on such details as the minimum number of days of school per year, and even on the requirements for teacher certification. But in other respects which we will discuss presently, agreement may be infinitely more difficult.

THE OBSTACLES TO FEDERAL AID FOR EDUCATION

The need for federal aid to public education has been recognized as acute for at least three decades. During this period research studies have reported in complete detail the financial abilities and the educational needs of the states. The professional study devoted to the situation probably has been as thorough as for any problem in education. There can be little doubt, either, of the ability of the American people to supply, through their federal government, adequate funds for the educational requirements of the states. Neither awareness of need nor ability to finance the program has delayed a large-scale plan for federal aid to education.

Numerous attempts have been made to secure passage of federal legislation to provide financial aid to the states. Bills for this purpose have been introduced in session after session of Congress, but up to the present time no legislation providing *general* financial aid has been passed. Only those bills which offered funds for such *specific* purposes as vocational education and hot lunch programs have been successful.

The real difficulties in enacting federal legislation for financial aid of a more general nature do not grow out of any questions of state need or federal ability to pay. Two issues in the use of federal funds for education within the states have so divided opinion that it has been impossible to secure passage of the legislation. One of these crucial issues is whether federal funds shall be used within the states for the support of segregated schools. The other is the question of whether federal funds shall be used for the support of private religious schools.

The school systems are "integrated" in most of the states. White and Negro children can, and do, attend the same public schools. However, a substantial minority of the states still maintain segregated school systems in which the two races are educated in separate buildings. Both practices have been reflected in congressional refusal to provide federal funds that either could be used to *maintain* segregation or, on the other hand, that *could not* be used to aid schools still practicing segregation.

Since May 17, 1956, we now have, of course, the momentous Supreme Court decision declaring segregation of the races in public schools as unconstitutional. Yet since even this has not yet ended the practice of segregation, it is to be expected that opposition to federal aid to education will continue for some time. However, with both morality and legality now on the side of the unsegregated school, opposition to federal aid to education on this score, at least, should gradually diminish.

The issue of financial support for the parochial schools presents an even more stubborn problem for the enactment of federal legislation for the equalization of educational opportunity among the states. In this area there has been no definitive pronouncement comparable to the Supreme Court decision on segregation. Up to now, congressional opposition to unrestricted federal aid to the states has been adamant. Since some of the states now provide funds for parochial schools for such items as textbooks and bus transportation, it has been presumed that any federal funds received in those states would be used in the same manner. Opposition to such unrestricted use of federal grants has been very active.

On the other hand, opposition to the allocation of federal funds which could *not* be used to aid the parochial schools has also been too strong to permit the enactment of legislation. In effect, the opposing forces have been stalemated. Neither the bills which would enable the parochial schools to share in federal funds, nor the bills which would exclude them have been able to muster enough support to be passed. As far as can now be foreseen, the stalemate is likely to continue.

THE EFFECTS OF LACK OF MONEY UPON LEARNING

The final consideration in problems of school finance, as in all other school matters, must be the effect upon the quality of our children's learning. Some things that are learned are as precisely definable as the spelling of a word, a simple sum in arithmetic, or the date of the Continental Congress. Others, such as the ability to comprehend the meaning of a paragraph or to think through the writing of an essay, can be formulated only in more general terms. And still others, by no means any less useful, are even more intangible. These latter concern a person's ability to adjust to his own experiences and to life in general. All of these types of learning, as well as many others, add up to overall behavior patterns which in large measure are the results of education.

Children's learnings come from experiences of many kinds in many places. The school is but one of a number of educative institutions, but it is the only one which is both an organized and a public institution. No other social institution in our society possesses both of these characteristics. The home, the church, and the organizations for children and youth all are regarded highly for their educational purposes, but none of them is as exclusively and specifically an institution for the formal education of the nation's children as is the public school.

Differences in financial support cannot but affect conditions in the schools, and thereby, the learnings of children. In general, the greater the financial resources, the better the education. In specific cases, however, it may be found that a local school district has concentrated on one aspect of its educational program to make it superior to others. This sort of contrast is seen more frequently in athletics and music than in the other phases of the school program. A fine gymnasium or band, in a relatively poor community with generally meager school offerings, is much more common than a fine school library or science laboratory under similar economic circumstances.

The venerable folk saying that anyone who wants to can learn in spite of poor teachers and equipment contains some truth, but is not a useful guide in the organization and administration of public education. Undoubtedly, an eager student can learn a great deal on his own, even under poor conditions, but just as surely he could learn much more with better opportunities. The facts must be faced, also, that a good many children are not particularly eager. They not only need to learn, but they also need to learn to want to learn, and this is an educational problem that necessitates the best in teaching and equipment.

It is hardly fair to expect one community's children to learn as much and as well under inferior conditions as another city's children learn under much better circumstances. One of the strongest arguments that can be made for reducing financial inequalities among school districts is essentially humanitarian: All children deserve as nearly equal opportunities to learn as can be designed for them.

Nor is it fair for some states to continue to export their wealth to other states in the form of educated graduates of their public schools. There should be a two-way exchange of wealth in which funds enter a state to be used in the education of persons who will later leave. In such an exchange, the states which regularly attract youth from other areas would share in the expenses of educating their own future citizens. It makes no practical difference that it is not possible to identify in advance all of the youth who will leave, since it is certain that an approximate and predictable percent will migrate from certain states to other states.

Admittedly a considerable interchange of graduates now occurs among the states, and the wealth invested in their education thus flows back and forth across state boundaries. However, in the case of the primarily rural states, the migration is very nearly a one-directional flow. They lose by export many times the number of graduates they can expect to attract from other states.

SOCIETY'S INVESTMENT IN EDUCATION

From the standpoint of the society's total investment in education, present conditions in which the geographical accidents of birth insure better schools for some of the nation's future citizens than for others are indefensible. Here the argument for equalizing educational opportunities through federal aid to schools is based on the principle that the welfare of the nation as a whole depends upon the circumstances under which all of its citizens are educated. No city or state can really afford the serious social and economic problems which result from an influx of poorly educated adults and their children. Only with the greatest difficulty can such new residents be absorbed into the city's accepted patterns of work, housing, education, and recreation. Most of this country's large cities have been confronted with these difficulties for years. The most promising solution to these problems, and the least expensive in the long run, is more better-quality education in the areas from which the migrants have been attracted. Although the cities are now paying heavily in emergency programs for the lack of education among their immigrants, the most they can hope to realize from such expenditures is to keep abreast of the incoming tide. Education offers the hope of alleviating the problem at its source.

A society which invests in public education must also concern itself with identifying and developing the talents of its young. The fact that large numbers of children with fine potential abilities do not realize them has been well known among educators for many years, although it has seemed recently to be news to many critics of the schools. Thousands of students who leave the school forever with mediocre records at high-school graduation, or even before, started with the learning capacity to succeed in college. Others of average or below normal ability often fail to attain their potentials in the school. The most tragic of all are the cases in which high ranking high-school graduates cannot afford to go to college. Whatever the student's level of ability, failure to work up to it is a waste of human talent. The achievement of children and youth in the schools is influenced by many factors, but one of the most important is the quality of the education that is available for them there. The abilities of its young people is one of the nation's most precious resources. Their fullest development in every part of every state is the responsibility of the entire country.

The financing of the public schools at any given time must be evaluated by its effectiveness in meeting the needs for public education in our democracy. At this time financing is deficient in meeting those needs both within the states and among the states. Persistent efforts have been made to equalize educational opportunities within the states, and much progress has resulted from those efforts. In comparison, only little has been done to ameliorate inequalities among the states. A substantial program of federal aid to education would accelerate the progress of equalization within all but the wealthiest states where the public schools are at their best.

Despite the serious inequalities presented in this chapter, the United States has approached more nearly the ideal of free public education for everyone than any other country in the world. More children and more youth, both in numbers and percentages, attend school for more years in this country than anywhere else. Yet in some respects our schools are not completely free. It will be the purpose of the next chapter to examine the costs of attending the public schools and to explore some of the social and economic factors which make these expenses important in the quality of the education American children receive.

7. The Unrealized Ideal of the Free Public School

The American public school is a magnificent democratic achievement, a monument to the will and generosity of a free citizenry. At times, the American people have supported their public schools directly, through local elections for bond issues and the raising of the mill levy. On other occasions, they have expressed their wishes to support education through their elected representatives, as members of local school boards or state legislatures.

At the present time, the public school is the "ladder of opportunity" for all American children. Accessible to every community are locally-administered, tuition-free public elementary and secondary schools. Within a few miles of the homes of most American youth are public institutions of higher education in which the tuition paid covers but a fraction of the cost of actual operations. Since most public colleges and universities are located in or near populous urban centers, a very large number of students can live at home while attending them. Only a small percentage of the country's youth reside any great distance from a state institution of higher education.

In spite of its accessibility, however, the American educational ladder remains much more difficult to climb for some people than for others. Indeed, a good many of our youth find its ascension next to impossible. There are two chief reasons for this. One is the obvious fact that children with low intellectual ability simply cannot measure up to all the educational opportunities available to them through the public educational curricula. The other and socially more significant concerns the economic position of the child's family. For the fact is that although the public schools are tuition-free, the expenses of attending them bear so heavily upon many American families that it is difficult for their children even to complete high school. For them, the free school is not free enough, and the ideal of a free public education often cannot be realized.

THE FAMILY'S ECONOMIC POSITION

The people of the United States have achieved a level of material prosperity without precedent. In the years since World War II, the expansion of the national economy has exceeded even the most optimistic expectations. It is estimated that the gross national product of goods and services will soon reach the round total of five hundred billions of dollars per year. This vast sum is evidenced in such visible forms as new homes, appliances, cars, and farm machinery.

Despite the unprecedented level of national prosperity, however, the population has not benefited uniformly. A very large number of American families cannot share in the enjoyment of new cars and new homes because their incomes have been too low to afford such purchases. As recently as 1957, about one quarter of all American families had annual incomes of less than $3,000. Their limited purchasing power virtually excluded them from the buying market for new homes and cars, as well as a great many other items. A slightly larger number of families received incomes in 1957 ranging from $3,000 to $5,000, a level at which the purchase of a new car or home is still very difficult. The total number of families with incomes below $5,000 in 1957 was twenty-three million, which amounted to a little more than 50 percent of all American families.

All of the costs of living are serious problems at to-day's prices for the family which has less than $5,000 per year. While an annual income of $5,000 may once have permitted a pleasant margin of luxury, it can now suffice for little more than the basic necessities. Any addition to family expenditures must usually mean doing without another item.

There is no reason to believe that low-income families plan their buying any more wisely than those who have more money to spend. Most families of all degrees of prosperity sometimes make questionable purchases, but such errors in planning are most serious for the families with low incomes, and the lower the income the more crucial the error. The high-income family can afford to budget itself casually and to make purchasing errors, for only a portion of its income needs to be committed to the basic costs of living. Yet in the case of the many other families who must expend all their receipts to defray the cost of essentials, there is no such margin of comfort. For these people, therefore, even the modest outlays attendant on their children's going to school may present serious problems.

THE COSTS OF ATTENDING THE PUBLIC SCHOOLS

The tuition-free public school is not completely free. There are innumerable small expenses connected both with the children's academic work as well as with their other activities in the school. Occasionally, even some larger purchases may be needed. The total expenditures for one child for a year can amount to a respectable sum, even in these days of seeming prosperity for all.

The need for books and supplies confronts parents at the very beginning of the school year. A textbook for each course, along with pens, pencils, notebooks, and paper, represents the minimum outlay. Sometimes more than one book is needed for a course, and other items of supply, as for example, crayons or paints, may also be needed. All of these things are musts for every child. A considerable variation in cost is possible for such items as pens and notebooks, which often are expensive enough to be regarded as luxury items.

A strong trend has developed to reduce costs to parents by providing free textbooks at public expense. This has become the practice in many states, and in some communities in other states. Often, elsewhere, the textbooks are rented to students at a fraction of their cost, so that they will be paid for after they have been used four or five times. Both of these practices reduce the direct costs to parents substantially, but many schools still require students to furnish their own books. Nearly everywhere, pupils must still buy needed supplies, many of which present recurring costs as they are used up and replaced. Parents are met with small, but steady expenses for such new items as pencils and paper.

As with nearly all other items the family purchases, the cost of school books and supplies has risen. A book the parent bought for $1.60 in his own high-school days now costs $4.00. The price of a popular mechanical pencil, which once sold for 10 cents, has been increased to 39 cents. Everything is more expensive than when Dad went to school.

The costs of attending school increase as the child moves up through the grades. Textbooks are more expensive. New items appear on the student's lists of needs, particularly in the secondary school: uniform dresses for homemaking courses, uniforms and shoes for physical education, laboratory fees for science courses, and various materials for work in the shop.

THE PAY ASSEMBLY

Not all of the expenses of attending the public school originate in the classes. The "pay assembly" has been developed into a profitable and dependable source of funds in many high schools. It is used as follows: A student club which needs to raise money to carry out its plans for the year, secures permission from the administration to sponsor an assembly during one of the regular daily periods. The entertainment may be a rented film or some "live" talent. Everyone who buys a ticket is excused from class to go to the assembly, and usually nearly everyone does buy a ticket. If the price of admission is set at twenty-five cents, and if the entertainment costs no more than twenty-five dollars, the net yield from such a student function may easily exceed two hundred dollars. It is, indeed, about as near to an effortless means of raising funds as can be found. While critics of the pay assembly have asked whether the sponsoring club is selling the assembly program or the privilege of getting out of class, the practice continues widely. It must be recorded to the credit of a number of high-school principals that they have put a stop to it. Yet where it still persists, it is a steady drain on students' pockets.

EXTRACURRICULAR ACTIVITIES ADD EXPENSES

Extracurricular activities are more numerous in the secondary school than in the elementary grades, and these add to the costs of attending school as the student grows older. One type of regular expense is incurred in attending school parties and athletic contests, which are held at least once a week in a large and busy high school. To the cost of a ticket to the party or game must be added the prices of hot dogs, popcorn, candy, and soft drinks to satisfy adolescent appetites. Often these amount to more than the price of the ticket, yet it is very hard for parents to refuse the request when "everybody else buys them." The alternative, which many youths of low-income families in fact cannot avoid, is to stay away from the party or game altogether.

Another type of expense is incurred by students who participate in the many extracurricular activities. Often special items of equipment and supplies are needed for athletics and dramatics. Athletic uniforms are universally furnished free of cost to the student, but while a great many high schools provide such minor essentials as the shoes and socks for their teams, squad members in other schools are required to pay part or all of the costs of these items. Participation in a school play may cost the student nothing for personal expenses, or it may begin with the purchase of clothing and end with

an elaborate party for the members of the cast. Participation in either athletics or dramatics takes a great
many hours in which the student could be earning
money in a part-time job. The loss of potential earning
power during these hours must be reckoned as another
cost of attending the school. It is an expense which
must be considered seriously by many; local surveys
have shown that as many as half the students of a city
high school work at part-time jobs.

LARGER PURCHASES

Occasional large expenses may occur as early as the
middle grades of the elementary school. These are in
addition to the regular costs involved in classes and extracurricular activities. A very common example is the
purchase of a musical instrument. Although these are
furnished in some schools, or rented at a low fee, many
others require the student to buy his own.

CLASS PARTIES AND GRADUATION

The annual junior and senior parties are in a category
all by themselves. Often each prom is expected to be more
elaborate and costly than the last. Even though class
funds have been raised in the course of the year to take
care of such items as the orchestra and decorations, a
boy's expenses for the evening may easily run to twenty
or thirty dollars, without figuring in the cost of new
clothing. A tankful of gasoline, an orchid corsage, and
the long-anticipated visit to a night club after the prom
are often regarded as necessary parts of the evening's
entertainment. It is small wonder that so many students
do not find it convenient to attend.

The proud occasions on which communities gather annually to honor their high-school graduates are also expensive affairs for parents. At the very least, the commencement exercises are bound to involve expenses for various items of new apparel—although it may be rationalized that the new clothing would have been needed anyway. Where no effort has been made to keep down the expenses of graduation, they often go far beyond moderation.

The pressures of conformity to group expectations compel the seniors in many high schools to purchase graduation announcements and calling cards. Few people now participate in the social routines for which calling cards are appropriate, but the seniors still buy them. Most graduates also feel the need for photographs, and these, too, are expensive. The custom of exchanging them with one's friends is pleasant, but at the price of thirty-five dollars per dozen, which is not unusual, the exchange means that the parents are paying nearly three dollars for each of the portraits of Junior's friends that ornament the mantel for a few days before they are packed away into obscurity. All in all, the total costs of clothing, announcements, cards, photographs, and graduation parties can come to as much as $200 per student. Needless to say, not all of the graduates' parents spend as much as this. But for those who do—and even for those who do only in part—the financial drain is very considerable indeed.

AN EXPENSIVE LADDER

The educational ladder of opportunity is an expensive climb. The child's progress through the public schools confronts the parents with one occasion after another at which money is needed. The items of expense mentioned above are by no means a complete listing. The parents of almost any high-school senior could add numerous additional costs. For example, neither the class ring nor the school yearbook has been mentioned. Often the total costs of attending the public school amount to $100 per year or more in the upper grades, and this is climaxed by another large outlay at the time of graduation from the high school.

The expenses of attending school are multiplied for families with several children of school age. Only simple arithmetic is needed to figure the costs for the family with two or three teen-agers attending the high school at the same time. The total expenses for a freshman, a sophomore, and a senior may easily reach $400 or $500 for a single year if all of them participate fully in the school's program of events and activities.

It is exceedingly difficult, and often impossible, for low-income families to manage school expenses amounting to ten or fifteen percent of their annual income. Yet this can be the situation for a family with a $4,000 income and three children attending a typical high school. Usually the family income cannot be stretched to include all of the expenses of the school, and so the children do not participate fully in the school's program. Their lack of such participation undoubtedly lessens what they get out of their education.

PARTICIPATION OF STUDENTS FROM LOW-INCOME FAMILIES

Lack of full participation in the school program is most common among children of low-income families. It is much less frequent among students of middle and high social and economic status. For the latter non-participation is usually a matter of choice, whereas those of low income often simply cannot afford to participate.

The school is but one of many sets of interrelated experiences in the lives of American children. Family experiences and attitudes which children bring to school with them, and over which the school has little or no control, are no less important as factors affecting the quantity and quality of an individual's education. In the context of this discussion let us examine some of the details of these various educational experiences as they are related to the levels of family income. While the economic situation of the family is by no means the only responsible factor, it can be presumed to exercise a very considerable effect. Attention will be given first to the relationship of the quantity of education received to the financial circumstances of the family, and then to similar relationships in connection with the quality of education.

THE NUMBER OF YEARS OF SCHOOL COMPLETED

The most obvious index of the quantity of education is the number of years of school completed by an individual. At the present time approximately one-half of all the children who enter the public schools continue their attendance until they are graduated from the high school. The other half withdraw at some point before the completion of the twelfth grade. It seems extremely significant that the great majority of the "drop outs" are of low social-economic status. A large number of them also represent minority ethnic groups, membership in which is often accompanied by low social and economic rank. Occasionally a child from a middle-income family does withdraw from the school, but the percentages are very low. Cases of withdrawal among the sons and daughters of high-status families are extremely rare. The conclusion can hardly be avoided that the average number of years of school attendance is closely related to the social and economic positions of students' families.

The family's expectations for its children obviously extend to their education. In a home where every adult member of the family has been graduated from high school, and where it is expected that every child will do the same, high school completion is nearly automatic. In a different sort of family, representing the other extreme in educational traditions, there may be not a single adult who has remained in school long enough to receive a diploma. Here, family expectations do not include graduation from high school, and it will be difficult for any of the children to be the first to accomplish it.

Family expectations are related to social and economic status. High educational expectations are characteristic of families of middle- and high-income levels, while low expectations typically accompany low incomes. These, of course, are generalities to which there are many exceptions. But the exceptions are nearly always those in which high expectations are to be found in low-income families. Almost never do the low expectations occur in families of middle or high status. And the percentages of drop outs follow the general tendencies rather than the exceptions.

STUDENT PARTICIPATION IN ACTIVITIES

Another useful measure of the quantity of education received in the school is the extent to which students take part in extracurricular activities. The activities of the high school have been chosen for illustration instead of those of the elementary grades for two reasons: (1) the high school program is much more extensive; (2) the expenses of belonging and participating are much higher in the secondary school. Not only are the activities themselves more expensive, but the time spent in them has more earning potential for high-school students than for younger boys and girls. Disregarding, for the moment, any question of their quality, figures on the number of activities in which high-school students take part show some interesting relationships to the economic level of the family.

The average number of individual memberships in extracurricular activities in high schools tends to vary directly with the social and economic status of the students' family. In general, save for such obvious exceptions as the boy of lower-class background who has outstanding athletic abilities, the lower the status of the family, the fewer the activities in which the student participates.

The same general pattern of participation in the high school's activities holds for spectator attendance as well as for belonging to organizations. The sons and daughters of lower-class families go to few of the high school's games, parties, and plays. Knowledge of families' positions on the community's economic scale enables us to predict with great accuracy which students will take part in activities, either as members or spectators. Almost all educators now consider extracurricular activities to be essential parts of the modern curriculum. From this widely-accepted viewpoint, students who do not take part in them miss important phases of the education the public school attempts to offer.

On the average, the children of low-income families actually receive smaller quantities of education in the public schools than those of families of middle- and high-income levels. They tend to be in school for fewer years, and their programs for those years are less extensive. These are measures of quantity, and while one may surmise that differences in quality also appear, one cannot be certain without making some study of them. But some useful research has been done on this topic, and its results show interesting general relationships between school success and family prosperity.

DIFFERENCES IN QUALITY AS WELL AS QUANTITY

The most convenient measure of the quality of an education is the grade the student receives in a subject. While it must be acknowledged that school marks have been shown to be lacking in complete accuracy, nevertheless they are the teachers' judgments of the quality of their pupils' work, and they have the advantage of being readily accessible to anyone who wishes to look at them.

Where studies have been made of the distribution of school grades according to the social and economic status of children's families, close relationships have been found between them. Average grades are higher for those from high-income families, and the decreases in grade averages are consistent with the differences in family prosperity. Grade averages are lowest of all for those students who come to the school from the lowest economic strata of the community. These are the general patterns into which the grades of most students fit.

There was a time when some people might have been tempted to explain such patterns in grade averages by suggesting that they followed from differences in intelligence, assuming that intelligence corresponds roughly to inherited position in the social and economic scale of the community. But anyone who has studied the problem thoroughly would now vigorously deny such an explanation. It is more probable that great differences in intelligence occur among individuals of all economic levels, and that these differences are not associated with social and economic status.

The best explanation of the relationship of grade averages to social and economic status is to be found in the complex factors of the child's social conditioning. A myriad of experiences shapes his attitudes, abilities, and interests about the potentials he has inherited. His conditioning influences his ambitions and expectations, ideals and standards, and beliefs and loyalties. Experiences in the school are phases of the conditioning, and behavior in the school exhibits the personal qualities which have developed. The actual level of behavior cannot be above inherited potential abilities, but it can be anywhere from a little below to very far below. One of the factors which influences the level of behavior is the economic situation of the student's family. Students from low-status families tend to bring to the school less than the average desire to achieve.

When students who have dropped out of the high school before graduation have been asked why they withdrew, they have given many reasons. Among those most frequently mentioned are two which clearly have economic origins: (1) that they preferred work to school and that they needed money for themselves and their families; (2) that they lacked interest in the school work. It is easily understandable that youths who feel that they must earn money for personal and family needs should display little interest in subjects which offer financial rewards only in the distant future. The quality of the individual's education thus tends to be affected by the same factors of family economics which limit its quantity.

THE VIEWPOINT OF FOLKLORE

The problems of furnishing free public schools for all American children involve complex social and economic factors. The preceding pages of this chapter presented the broad outlines of the family's economic position, the costs of attending the public schools, and the participation of students from low-income families. Much is known about these factors because a large amount of data has been gathered in studying them. The accumulated knowledge stands in contrast to the unverified assumptions of the folklore of public education.

One of the most strongly held folk beliefs opposes reducing the costs of attending public schools, for this cherished bit of dogma holds that people really appreciate only the things for which they are required to pay. One hears the exponents of this belief say that children will not take as good care of free books as those they have to buy. In this argument, the book is the symbol of all the other equipment and supplies used in the schools, and appreciation is considered to apply to all of them along with the book. Presumably, free equipment and supplies would have unfortunate effects on the character of children—they would not learn to take good care of these things. The ultimate step in following this principle to its conclusion would be to abolish the public schools altogether. Then every family would pay privately for all education, and children would overflow with appreciation.

It is quite natural for children to handle free items carelessly, even to the extent of damaging or losing them. But it is also natural for them to treat items their parents have purchased for them in just the same way. Every parent and teacher has had many opportunities to observe the different attitudes children exhibit toward their personal possessions. Such items of apparel as caps, jackets, and overshoes frequently remain for months in the "lost and found" box in the principal's office, waiting to be claimed by their owners who seem to have had no appreciation of them even though they were paid for by their parents. Other children show great concern for these and other possessions.

Probably, concern for one's personal property has little relationship to who paid for it; other factors seem more important. Among these factors are the learnings from parents and other adults as well as from other children, learnings of what a person is supposed to do with his property. In some children's groups, lack of responsibility and care will actually enhance personal prestige. All of these learnings come in the general processes of social conditioning, that is, of growing up in a society. The folk belief that people "appreciate what they pay for" singles out one of many factors to the neglect of others which are more useful in understanding human behavior. When followed in school administration, as it undoubtedly is in many American communities at this time, the belief hurts both the quantity and the quality of the education of a very large number of American children.

THE AMOUNT OF EDUCATION IS RELATIVE

How important education may be to a particular child is a relative thing. It depends at least in part upon how much education other children have received. After all, those who drop out of high school before graduation still have had more years of schooling than most of the population received only a few generations ago. And similarly, even meager participation in today's extracurricular activities is more than high-school students of the last century enjoyed. But since we must consider the educational needs of our youngsters in the light of present school populations, the continuing, enormous differences in both the quantity and quality of our public education cannot but be a matter of deep concern.

Perhaps in some earlier American communities the populations were sufficiently homogeneous in occupations and economic circumstances that the costs of attending school had approximately the same effect on all local young people. It is conceivable that in some small rural communities all families were on about the same financial level. In such hypothetical circumstances, whether the family paid the expenses of attending the school privately and directly, or whether it did so publicly (and indirectly) through taxes would make little difference in the length and quality of the education received. But no such situations exist in today's American communities. Differences among families in economic status are characteristic of our contemporary society, and these differences are reflected quite closely in the education our children receive. The folk belief that people feel responsible only for what they have purchased privately ignores the many tragic deficiencies in the education of large numbers of American youngsters, deficiencies stemming, in part at least, from the costs of attending the public schools.

A TEST OF INDIVIDUAL BELIEFS

The idea of a tuition-free public school open to all children is a comparatively new one in the history of civilization. In earlier days only a few children attended formal schools, and those who did paid privately for their education. Our own public schools go much farther toward providing free universal education than has even been contemplated in most countries.

School administration now appears to be moving toward freer schools by reducing some of the costs of attendance. Whether such trends are to continue will depend upon the attitudes of those who support the public schools with their taxes, for the wishes of the majority will eventually determine school policies in this respect as in others.

The reader can test his own feelings about paying the costs of the public schools from public funds by considering his willingness to have all equipment and supplies provided free of charge for all children. He might begin by considering such items as free textbooks and free transportation for all children who live beyond a reasonable walking distance. Both are very commonly furnished by school districts at the present time. Then he might consider free admission to all of the school's athletic contests and free yearbooks. Neither is commonly furnished at present. He might finally contem-

plate free uniforms and shoes for the physical education courses, both of which have almost never been
provided by the schools.

Anyone can very easily assemble a list of a dozen or
more such items. If he responds affirmatively to many
of them, he must realize that he thereby expresses his
willingness to commit the school to a substantial increase
in expenditures. Some of the items will involve less
expense than others, but the least of them will amount
to several dollars for each student for a school year, and
one cannot go very far down the list before reaching an
annual sum of $100 or more per student.

Whatever the amount to which a person is willing to
commit himself, it can be no more than parents are now
asked to pay privately if they wish their children to
participate fully in the school program. Willingness to
bear the expenses publicly is willingness to shift the
burden from private incomes, where it is often an un-
bearable load, to public resources. If this could be made
possible, a large increase in participation, causing still
more public expense, should be anticipated, for a great
many students who cannot now afford the costs would
then be able to take part in more activities for more
years of school. Yet the additional expense would be a
sound investment in better education for millions of
contemporary and future children.

Much of this chapter has been concerned with the
costs of attending the public high school, and it has
been shown that the pressures of these costs affect the
learning of many of the students. But the high school
presents other problems which are also critical, and in
which the results of careful analysis are also often ob-
scured by folk beliefs which have grown up with the

institution. Chapter VIII will give consideration to both the problems and the folklore of the American high school.

8. Facts and Fictions of the American High School

In the fifty years from 1890 to 1940, increases in American high-school enrollment far exceeded all precedents in the history of education. In 1890, there were some 360,000 students enrolled in the high schools of the United States, approximately 7 percent of the total of high-school age youth. In each of the next five decades, American high-school enrollment nearly doubled. By 1940 the figure had reached a total of some 7,100,000 students, almost 19 times the enrollment of 1890. It is true, of course, that this rise is to some extent a reflection of increases in the population in general. The number of high-school age youth, for example, increased some 80 percent during these decades. Yet even when this is allowed for, the fact remains that by 1940, more than 70 percent of Americans in this age group were enrolled in high schools—as compared with 7 percent in 1890.

High-school enrollment decreased slightly during the war years of the early 1940's as youth left school to enter the armed services and employment. Thereafter it rose again until it now stands at a peak of more than 8,000,000. However, the growth in enrollment in the 1950's has been very largely due to increases in the nation's youth population. The period of rapid increase in the percent of enrollment ended about 1940.

The tremendous growth in high-school enrollment was accompanied by vast changes in the composition of the student body. The high school of 1890 was a highly selective educational institution, attended by only one of every fourteen youth. Graduation was an achievement that only a small percent of the adults of that period could boast. By 1940, most of the high school's selective character had disappeared, and seven of every ten youth were enrolled. The American high school had become an institution of mass education.

CHANGES IN AMERICAN LIFE

The period from 1890 to 1940 saw also a great many other striking transformations in American life: the introduction of mass technology, the advent of the automobile, radio and the airplane, and perhaps most significant of all, the steadily burgeoning material expectations of the American people.

All the while, of course, were occurring equally significant changes in the social sphere. The dominant role of the American male gradually declined; the relations between the sexes for the first time began to approach something like equality; more and more women entered the labor market; and as this happened, various new social patterns began to develop.

Legislation in the early years of the twentieth century also changed the status of children and youth by limiting their availability to the labor market. Restrictions were placed on the kinds of work they were permitted to do and the number of hours they could be employed. Full-time, continuous employment was prohibited until late adolescence.

The American family ceased to be a unit of production and became almost entirely dependent for its needs upon the earning power of one or more of its members. Items which earlier American families had made or grown for themselves were now purchased through intricate and specialized systems of manufacture and distribution.

All of these changes contributed to the rapid increase in high-school enrollments. Women, if they wished to utilize their new independence, required more education. Thousands of jobs, newly created for both men and women, called for more education. Children, legally protected from exploitation, were freed for more years of schooling.

THE VARIED NEEDS OF YOUTH

The American high school of 1890 could expect to satisfy nearly all of its patrons by performing one function reasonably well. If its graduates were prepared to enter college, the high school had served its purpose. The needs of those students who were not bound for college were either ignored or presumed to be equally well met by the same curriculum that prepared for higher education. Preparation for college was considered by the nation's most articulate educators to be the best preparation for all students, college bound or not. The high school of that era was required to offer only a college preparatory curriculum to a relatively small number of youth.

In contrast, the high school of 1940 and today is expected to offer all things for all youth. Demands for college preparation are still strong, but such an education can no longer be considered adequate for students who will not go on to college. For these boys and girls, general and vocational education has been insistently advocated.

Mass education on the secondary level presents individual and group needs which cannot be met by college preparatory curricula alone. Now that all youth are expected to attend school, the ranges of student interests and abilities are much greater than half a century ago, when only one of fourteen was enrolled in the high school. Some youth cannot do the formal work of the college preparatory curriculum. Some who could do it have other interests. For a long time, this situation has been apparent to most of the principals and teachers of our secondary schools, but it has been generally ignored by those who cherish the folklore of education.

THE FOLKLORE OF THE HIGH SCHOOL

Educational folk lore continues to view the contemporary high school as though it still served only the same kind of secondary school population as in 1890. More specifically, it still holds the sole function of the secondary school to be academic preparation for higher education.

In actual fact, of course, this view is a misleading anachronism. It ignores basic educational needs not only of those students who do *not* go on to college, but also of those who do. Most importantly, it fails to consider the need of all types of youngsters to learn as much as possible about themselves and their relationship with others. Yet as we know, adequate training in this area of self-understanding and relationship to the community is no less vital for present-day young people than are the more academic aspects of education. And this is true of all of our youth, whether college-bound or not.

Most seriously neglected by the college preparatory curriculum are the needs of those students who do not continue their formal education beyond high school. For these, academic-type learning should be but one of a number of educational objectives. It can be argued that for those who go on to college and professional school, such subjects as foreign languages, history, mathematics, and science are, in effect, in the nature of vocational training. But this is certainly not the case for the millions of terminal high-school students. Since these latter are headed for very different kinds of careers, they require a very different kind of vocational education.

THE INFLUENCE OF THE COLLEGE UPON THE HIGH SCHOOL

Glorification of the college has interfered seriously with the development of the American high school. It has subordinated high school to the role of preparing students for later education that is still to follow, when in reality the high school's proper task is much more independent and complex.

The influence of the college may be recognized in a number of contemporary high-school practices. Perhaps the most obvious is the appearance in the high-school curriculum of courses which originated in the college. Among these are the most familiar of the high-school subjects, those which are commonly required of all students—English, history, the languages, the sciences, and mathematics. Two of the newer college disciplines, psychology and sociology, recently have been introduced as subjects in high school, where they are growing more and more popular. The high school has originated only a few of its subjects, and these have tended to remain on the fringe of the curriculum.

The strength of the college's influence is also shown by the universal high-school practice of recording one unit of credit for each year's work in a subject. The unit of credit was originated about 1910 as a device to bring standardization into the records which high schools sent to the colleges. Its use spread rapidly until nearly all subjects were recorded in this manner, the chief exceptions being music and physical education for which one-fourth or one-half units are usually entered.

A curious, and often frustrating, effect of the unit system has been to make nearly all high-school subjects of uniform length. Shorthand and chemistry, United States history and general business, art and algebra, all are one-year courses. If one year is not enough, a second can be added, but seldom part of a second. Courses are never planned for two-thirds or 1-1/3 of a year for they would not fit into the unit pattern. Most high-school students take four, and only four, subjects, plus physical education and possibly music, as their year's work (though some schools go so far as to permit five subjects for more able students). Each subject is taught five days each week, completely occupying the hour of the day for which it has been scheduled. How educationally confining and frustrating this can be, no one knows better than the men and women who are responsible for planning the schedules of high-school students.

The colleges themselves do not use this system. They record course credits in different numbers of quarter or semester hours. College catalogs list courses ranging in credit from one to five hours, and students are permitted to combine different numbers of courses of different credit hours for totals which also differ. One student may register for five courses adding up to fourteen hours of credit, while another may put together four courses for a total of sixteen hours. A college student is free to use any given hour of the day, whether it be ten o'clock or two, for two courses of two or three hours each: one course on Tuesday and Thursday and another on Monday, Wednesday, and Friday.

The most curious aspect of the unit system is the fact that one institution has imposed upon another a system of scheduling courses and recording credits which it does not itself use, nor has ever contemplated using. The colleges were chiefly responsible for the introduction of the unit system into the American high school, but they have devised more flexible systems for their own use.

The American high school cannot hope to do its proper educational job when such important components of its program have been handed down from above. It is a situation without parallel at other levels in our educational system. High schools have not imposed their practices on junior high schools with the exception of the ninth grade, which was formerly included as the first year of the four-year high school. Scheduling practices in junior high schools differ from those in senior high schools in several important respects. They regularly schedule more than four subjects for their students, and they vary the length of their courses by arranging them for different numbers of periods per week. Junior high-school students often take seven or eight subjects, and some take even more. Junior high schools also combine two or more subjects into one long period much more frequently than do the senior high schools. Nor has the junior high school made any attempts to formulate a program for the elementary school. Both the elementary and the junior high schools have had much more freedom than the senior high schools to develop their own programs for their own students.

WHAT SHOULD THE HIGH SCHOOL LIBRARY BE?

Another illustrative result of the colleges' influence upon high schools can be observed in the latter's libraries. A prominent feature of the college library is its large reading room, accessible to students between classes and in the evening. Although high-school students are almost never free between classes, for in virtually all secondary schools they are required to attend study halls in the periods for which no classes appear on their schedules, and most high schools are locked up in the evenings, the typical high-school library closely resembles the reading room of the college library. Often it stands nearly empty, or is used as a study hall, through most of the school day.

What the high-school library should be, one can only conjecture. Who can say what it would be like if the library needs of youth had been studied and high-school libraries had been designed to meet them? Because *one* prominent feature of the college library has become the *entire* high-school library, it has been necessary to find means of using this learning aid of which the basic design was established before the needs of the students were considered.

Much the same can be said of most of the high-school subjects. Instead of beginning with questions of what youth most need to learn, teachers have had to struggle with the problems of adapting college subjects to the varied abilities and interests of high-school youth. Their efforts have resulted in real progress. Many changes have been introduced into the curriculum to make student experiences more interesting and more realistic. New content and new methods of presenting content have been introduced to revise or even replace older learning materials. A very substantial amount of reorganization has thus been effected in American secondary education in the first half of the twentieth century.

THE REORGANIZATION OF SECONDARY EDUCATION

Serious questioning of the merits of the college preparatory curriculum began more than forty years ago, when it became apparent that the function of the American secondary school needed to be modified and enlarged. As high-school enrollments steadily grew, it became ever clearer that for a great many of the new students the traditional preparation-for-college type of high-school education was neither suitable nor enough. For the first time, therefore, learning experiences began to be planned with a view to the actual needs and diversities of interest of American youngsters themselves. Soon a considerable professional literature on the subject of high-school reorganization appeared. And little by little, significant innovations began to be introduced into the traditional pattern of high-school subjects.

The reorganization movement stands in distinct con-

trast to the folk belief that high school is only preparation for higher education: it seeks to substitute learning experiences based upon accurate knowledge of
youth in their culture for uncritical acceptance of the
old, familiar sequences of courses. Answers are sought
to such questions as the following:

> What do young people need to learn about health?
> In what ways can young people best learn to be effective
> citizens in American democracy?
> How can young people be equipped to earn a living
> in the twentieth century?

It seems improbable that the reorganization of secondary education will ever go so far as to replace the
familiar high-school subjects with another framework
of learning experiences, although there are those who
have believed such sweeping revisions to be both necessary and possible. Most of the changes for which the
reorganization movement has been responsible have occurred within the old subjects (of which the original
names have been retained), or by adding new subjects
and services to the school curriculum.

The contents of the high-school courses in English,
for example, have been modified and expanded to
make the experiences of students more meaningful and
more useful. The organization of English as composition and literature is in the process of becoming the
language arts of reading, writing, speaking, and listening. Grammar is less frequently analyzed for its own
sake, and more often learned by and for use in situations
where children feel the need to communicate. Although
the familiar classics of literature are still read in a great
many high schools, they have been supplemented by a

rich variety of other readings, and some have been replaced by selections more appropriate to the interests of teen-agers. New English subjects now enrich the experiences of many students; in most large high schools the youth of today have opportunities to take elective courses in such aspects of English as speech, journalism, and dramatics.

The high-school guidance program is one of the most widely known and approved phases of the reorganization movement. It functions both within, and in addition to, the subjects in which students are enrolled. Within the prescribed learning experiences, there are many opportunities for teachers to aid students in recognizing the need for choices and in making the choices wisely. Other needs occur apart from the daily work in the classroom, and these are usually the province of the guidance specialist or counselor.

Parents of high-school students have been quick to realize the advantages in a guidance program. They have welcomed the school's assistance in planning choices among high-school courses, exploring career possibilities in relation to the students' unique abilities and interests, and choosing a college. They have also appreciated the school's aid in their adolescents' problems of personal and group behavior. In many communities parents have requested their local boards of education to add more guidance personnel in the secondary schools.

The basic intent of the reorganization movement has been to improve the high school's response to the needs of the present. The great formal disciplines of the colleges have not been neglected, for they are indispensable resources in the planning of the high-school curriculum, but they are now drawn upon selectively instead of exclusively. Their use is attuned to the known needs of American youth and the culture in which they live today. With this orientation, the reorganization movement has already accomplished great changes in the original college preparatory curriculum of the secondary school.

THE DIFFERENTIATED CURRICULUM

The reorganization of secondary education is a continuing process of adapting instruction and content to make them more effective. Since the specific problems of youth change as rapidly as the society in which they live, the task of reorganization can never be completed. New learning materials are produced regularly. Expansions of guidance and health services continue. Additions to the curriculum in the form of new subjects appear from time to time, although the elimination of the older courses is much less common. Their loss of popularity is evidenced by dwindling enrollments rather than by disappearance.

Despite the regularity of change in the curriculum, some general patterns of reorganization have been maintained. For example, there has been a trend toward differentiating offerings according to the special characteristics of each group of students. The trend is discernible within each of several of the secondary school departments, as well as in the establishment of separate curricula for different purposes. Accompanied by another important trend toward the study and guidance of pupils as individuals, the effect has been to enable high schools to fit their courses and curricula increasingly well to the known abilities and interests of their students. As with other aspects of the curriculum, the processes of differentiation are far from completely successful, but a substantial amount of real progress has been made.

High-school courses are commonly arranged into groups designated as specific curricula according to their purposes. Among the most prevalent are the college preparatory, the commercial, and the vocational. Somewhat less common are the agriculture, homemaking, and technical curricula. The purposes of all of these are described by their titles. High schools have very often added a general curriculum which is usually recommended for youngsters of uncertain purpose and less than average ability.

There is a considerable amount of overlapping among the several curricula, since all include the required courses in English, history, and physical education. However, differentiation frequently occurs within these stipulated requirements. In a great many high schools, English and history are taught on several levels of difficulty to match degrees of ability. They range from the college preparatory, which is the most difficult and thorough, down through several gradations to the courses which are designed for the general and vocational curricula. More than one college preparatory "track" is taught in some of the larger high schools. Where this happens, the top level may in the senior year culminate in the equivalent of college courses.

Differentiation also occurs in the high school's offerings in mathematics. For the college preparatory curriculum these consist of the traditional sequence of algebra, geometry and trigonometry, with the addition in the case of some of the larger high schools of analytics and calculus. For students who have chosen the commercial curriculum, there is provided a year's course in business arithmetic. And the students classified as "general" may meet their requirements by taking a course labeled general mathematics. In addition, there are often various other possible offerings. In some schools, for example, there may be a special course in shop mathematics, designed specifically for the vocational curriculum.

The contrasts among the differentiated curricula are most obvious in the subjects which are unique to each. The typical college preparatory curriculum includes several years of science and foreign languages. With its concentration on English, history, mathematics, science, and foreign languages, it is the most academic program the high school can offer. The commercial curriculum, as its name implies, differs from the others in its emphasis on such subjects as bookkeeping, typing, shorthand, and business machines. Quite different emphases appear in the vocational, agriculture, and homemaking curricula.

Differentiation may be achieved even without such a multiple-curricula type of organization. If a school is large enough to offer a sufficient number of courses, the schedules of individual students may be arranged according to the patterns described, even though separate curricula have never been designated. This is likely to happen where school officials have wished to avoid the appearance of rigidity sometimes conveyed by a set of curricula, each of which prescribes a specific list of subjects.

Now and then individual students register for certain subjects as electives which ordinarily are not included in their own curricula. For instance, college preparatory students often take a year of typing, and pupils in the commercial curriculum may wish to study a language.

Grade	COLLEGE PREPARATORY	COMMERCIAL — SECRETARIAL	COMMERCIAL — BOOKKEEPING	VOCATIONAL	GENERAL
Grade 9	English General Science Social Studies Algebra Language Physical Education	English General Science Social Studies General Business Elective Physical Education	English General Science Social Studies General Business Elective Physical Education	English General Science Social Studies General Mathematics Industrial Arts Physical Education	English General Science Social Studies General Mathematics Elective Physical Education
Grade 10	English Biology World History Plane Geometry Language Physical Education	English Biology Business Arithmetic Shorthand I Typing Physical Education	English Biology Business Arithmetic Typing Elective Physical Education	English Health Related Mathematics Mechanical Drawing Shop Physical Education	English Health World History Industrial Arts Physical Education
Grade 11	English Chemistry American History *Intermediate Algebra *Trigonometry Language Physical Education	English World History Shorthand and Transcription Business Law Elective Physical Education	English World History Bookkeeping I Business Law Elective Physical Education	English World History Related Science Mechanical Drawing Shop Physical Education	English Practical Science American History Elective Physical Education
Grade 12	English Physics World Problems *Solid Geometry *Advanced Algebra Elective Physical Education	English American History Secretarial Practice Elective Physical Education	English American History Bookkeeping II Business Machines Elective Physical Education	English American History *Related Mathematics *Related Science Shop Physical Education	English *Economics *Sociology Mechanical Drawing Elective Physical Education

This occasional practice adds yet another dimension to the extensive differentiation which characterizes the modern secondary school curriculum.

Students usually have their first opportunity to choose among elective subjects in the ninth grade. Up to that point, all have taken the same subjects, except for such courses as homemaking for the girls and industrial arts for the boys. As is to be expected, the youngsters receive all kinds of advice about their choices of courses. Other boys and girls, including big brothers and sisters, make many remarks about subjects and about teachers. Family expectations also influence the choices, although some parents show more concern than others at this stage of their children's education. The school's guidance people spend a great deal of time assisting students in making good selections of high-school subjects. Among the factors considered in this process are principally the recommendations of the child's teachers, the grades earned in seventh and eighth grade subjects, and scores on aptitude, achievement, and intelligence tests. But the guidance counselor can of course do no more than *recommend* courses. Youngsters and parents are free to disregard the school's recommendations of subjects and make their own choices. In most cases, however, the judgments of parents, youngsters, and counselors are in general agreement, for all of them work with the same information, and they usually work out the choices together.

Some typical high school curricula are shown in the chart on page 160. These are not exhaustive of the variations that may be offered and hence should be regarded only as examples. It must be borne in mind, too, that the ninth grade is often taken in the three-year junior high school.

The growth in the number and variety of extracurricular activities in the secondary school may be viewed as yet another phase of the movement toward reorganization. Their scope, especially in the large city high schools, is almost limitless; there, the number of activities may easily amount to forty or more. Some grow out of, and supplement the range of learnings of the regular high-school subjects. Examples of these are the foreign language, mathematics, science, and commercial clubs. Others have developed from the special interests of teachers and students, and bear little relationship to the regular courses. Among them are to be found such diverse activities as the Model Airplane and Rifle Clubs, the Rockhounds, and the Campers.

The most popular extracurricular activities, of course, and the most widely publicized are athletics and music. Because of the regular attention they receive, hardly anyone in an American community can remain unaware of them for long. But athletics and music differ from the rest of the extracurricular program only in the emphasis placed on them. They are similar to the other activities in that they too have emerged from the interests of the school and the community. The entire program of extracurricular activities illustrates a functional type of secondary education which has been developed in response to the needs and interests of youth living in American culture today. And in these activities are acquired some of the most useful learnings of the secondary school. The interests of students and teachers from which the extracurricular activities originated have become one of the most valuable phases of the curriculum.

Nothing is further from the truth than the often-repeated accusation that the modern high-school curriculum has been inflicted on the American public against their will and without their knowledge. Curriculum construction necessitates a long series of step-by-step repetitions of revisions and testing. Sudden and sweeping changes are almost never made.

The indisputable fact is that the new courses which have been introduced into the curriculum have been asked for by the parents. Since the early American secondary schools with their much sparser curricula, parents have demanded and obtained high-school courses in shop, homemaking, the commercial subjects, agriculture, art, physical education, music, and driver education, to name only a few. These subjects are not "fads and frills," as has so often been charged. They are legitimate courses of instruction which have been introduced in response to public demand. In theory, they can be eliminated from the curriculum at any time by the same sort of demand. Actually, the probability that the public will wish a return to the curriculum of 1890 is as remote as the likelihood that seventy years of invention and change in American life will be rolled back in a general return to the living conditions of the nineteenth century.

The general procedures by which new high-school courses are adopted make it virtually impossible for school officials to act against the public's will or without their knowledge. Although procedures vary somewhat throughout the country, the usual precondition for adding new courses is the approval of both the local board of education and the state department of public instruction. Since boards of education are composed of local citizens, and their meetings are open to the public, it is inconceivable that their decisions to add to the curriculum could long continue to go against the consensus of local public opinion. Moreover, any new course is very likely to be under consideration in a large number of communities at about the same time. Is credence to be given to the belief that the elected members of hundreds of local boards have secretly flouted the wishes of their neighbors in adding courses in art and music?

The public's chances of getting the curriculum they demand are always excellent. Just now, they are asking loudly for more attention to the needs of the most able students. Hundreds of high schools have already responded by offering courses on several levels of difficulty wherever this is feasible, and by teaching some of their subjects on the college level to their brightest seniors. These and other provisions for the best students are so impressive that they have been reserved for separate description in Chapter X.

THE DEPARTMENTALIZED SECONDARY SCHOOL

Millions of Americans have known only the departmentalized secondary school in which all teaching is by specialists in separate subjects. This form of curricular organization has been borrowed from higher education and has been accepted uncritically in most communities. In the great majority of today's secondary schools, all subjects are taught separately, and any relationships among their contents are left to the students to work out for themselves. After each of the six to eight periods of the day, the entire student body is reshuffled for the next period's classes. The typical student is in a different group for each of his classes and study halls. Surely no one should be surprised that so many of them feel lost in the shuffle.

Several very strong forces combine to perpetuate the departmentalized high school. Nearly always it is the only type of secondary school organization known to the community. Parents and older brothers and sisters have attended schools of this pattern. Practically all the teachers have studied in college departments and hence are trained to teach only in terms of the familiar, departmentalized subject schema. And state certification requirements for secondary school teachers also reinforce the departmental organization, since in most states high-school teachers are licensed to teach only the subjects in which they have specialized. All of these factors amount to intense, if unspoken, pressure to continue the existing departmentalization of secondary education. Indeed, many people have never even contemplated the possibility of any other type of high-school organization.

Yet in spite of the strongly conditioned attitudes favoring it, departmentalization has been increasingly questioned. Several hundred high schools have introduced modifications in which groups of students do remain together for two or more periods. By far the most common modification has been to combine one of the histories with one of the English courses. Usually some of the school's guidance functions are also included. This results in several distinct advantages: (1) materials of the two subjects supplement each other as, for

example, in American history and American literature;
(2) students and teachers have much better opportunities to get to know each other; (3) youngsters receive
more individual attention; (4) more diagnostic teaching is possible than when the teacher meets a different
class in each period; and (5) students also acquire more
ability to combine facts into general patterns of meaning, to see relationships among their learnings, and to
make sound judgments on problems which arise in
their study.

The name most frequently applied to the multiple-
period type of organization is the "core" curriculum,
although the use of the term "common learnings" is
spreading. These are general designations that include
a great variety of practices which are similar in their
objective: the unification of learnings. Core curricula
are slightly different in each school. They vary because
each is the local product of the planning within its own
institution. Formal influences, such as the textbook, for
example, have had little effect on the development of
the core curriculum, although the textbook is exploited
fully as a resource.

But the core is not the entire curriculum in any
school. Typically, it occupies from one-quarter to one-
half of the student's day, diminishing as the grade
level rises. Most of the high-school subjects retain their
identity even where all students take the core. While
English and the social studies are combined frequently, courses in the departments of mathematics, science, and the foreign languages remain as separate subjects.

The most common question which has been asked
about the core curriculum by those who have had no
first-hand experience with it is whether students learn

as much as when they take the conventional subjects in the departmental organization. Fortunately, enough testing has been done to make the answer clear: students learn slightly *more* subject matter in the core curriculum. Equally important, they learn more about working with other people and planning their own studies.

THE QUALITY OF LEARNING IS BETTER THAN EVER

One of the most common current criticisms of the high school is the charge that the quality of learning has declined. Horrible examples of graduates with very little academic knowledge are cited as proof that students do not learn as much as their predecessors did in earlier generations. The accusation is very likely to be coupled with an attack upon the modern curriculum, as though the critic supposes it to be the same for everyone.

The great range of student dissimilarities which has made necessary the differentiated curriculum must also be considered in appraising the quality of student learnings. Comparisons of the achievements of all of today's high-school population with those of the student body of 1890, for example, are wholly inappropriate, for they are comparisons of the more than 70 percent of the nation's youth who go to school today with the 7 percent who attended in 1890. Practically all of that student body possessed college preparatory abilities or interests. For a fair evaluation they can be compared with only the upper 10 percent of the modern high school's students. And if such a comparison were made, it would be found that high ranking students of sixty years ago would be no more than average among the

college preparatory seniors in any good high school today. The records of high-school achievement have been
similar to those in modern athletics; in both forms of
activity the performers have pushed their marks higher
and higher.

Students in curricula other than college preparatory
should be compared with the youth who "in the Good
Old Days" never even got as far as high school. Enrolled today in the commercial, agricultural, vocational
and general curricula, they are certainly learning a great
deal more both in their specialties as well as academi-
cally than did the corresponding young people of several generations ago.

The quality of learning in the modern high school
has by no means declined. If one compares contemporary students with earlier young people of corresponding abilities and interests one can only conclude
that it has, in fact, steadily improved.

THE SCHOOL DAY AND WORK EXPERIENCE

Full-time attendance is another common survival of
folklore in American secondary schools. Almost universally, students are required to be present in school for
all of their school careers. With rare exceptions, the
education of all students at a given school is planned to
be uniform in length. Although many young people
would profit more from a schedule in which practical
work experience was combined with school attendance,
particularly in the eleventh and twelfth grades, such
programs have been slow to emerge. They are available
now to only a very small percent of students.

It is true, of course, that large numbers of high-school
students have part-time employment outside the

school, but for nearly all of them the two experiences are wholly separate. Their work has no connection with the high school, and it is not considered to be part of their curriculum. Any mutual enrichment of academic subjects and employment happens only by accident— the same sort of accident that interrelates separate academic subjects for the student. It is to the credit of many high schools that their faculties assist students in finding jobs, but almost all of this is done outside the organization of the high-school curriculum.

The separation of school and work is but one phase of the isolation of the traditional high-school curriculum from American life. Separation from the family and the community are equally as complete. Far too often the graduate has had no planned assistance from his high school in understanding the three basic American institutions: work, family, and community. He leaves high school with only fragmentary, often erroneous, learnings about them.

But the American high school has changed and is changing. It is now neither what it was in the past nor what it will be in the future. An enormous amount of study has been given to its functions, and this will continue. The influence of the folklore will decline as more is learned by more people about the functions of the American high school, and as this knowledge is combined with understanding of the needs of youth in our culture. As this happens, the high school will attain its proper stature as a unique educational institution for all American youth.

The quality of learning in contemporary high schools has been mentioned only briefly in this chapter. Much more needs to be said on this topic with reference to both the secondary and the elementary schools, for the quality of learning has become a very popular point of attack in the welter of criticism against public education. More often than not, the charges are directed at the teaching of the fundamentals. Because of the frequency of such criticisms, and because they so often express the folk beliefs of education, they deserve careful attention. The question of what has happened to the fundamentals is to be the subject of the next chapter.

9. What Has Happened to the Fundamentals?

One way to generate a lively controversy in almost any group of adults is to ask a question about the teaching of the fundamentals in the modern public schools. Here is a topic on which a great many persons hold strong opinions which they are ready to express freely and at length. It is unnecessary to specify which fundamentals or which schools; only the mention of the word is enough to bring out an assortment of viewpoints, mostly negative. And what a tasty morsel for the hungry folklore advocates!

Such a discussion always includes the blunt statement, sometimes made in sorrow, often in indignation, that modern schools neglect teaching the fundamentals. Seldom is the assertion qualified by specific references —folklore deals chiefly in the broad and all-inclusive opinion in which all students in all schools are lumped together without regard for the large and real differences to be found among them. "They don't teach the fundamentals anymore"—this with the finality of a judge. Like so much of folklore, such a declaration is far too brief and simple to do justice to the complex problems of teaching and learning which are actually involved.

WHICH CHILDREN?

At the very outset of any earnest effort to ascertain how well the fundamentals are taught, it is necessary to get down to specifics. Which group of children are we talking about? And what kind of educational subject matter?

All of the variations in subjects that were described in Chapter II, and all the dissimilarities among children that were discussed in Chapter III, are of key relevance in determining the amounts of fundamentals which are taught and learned in the schools. The educational folklorist can ignore these complexities and content himself with the simple-minded notion of uniform children studying identical subjects. Whoever would give this matter serious attention must face up to their full importance.

At the lowest extremes of school performance, where lack of ability and opportunity are combined, are children who remain virtual illiterates into their teens. They cannot read even the simplest passages coherently; most of the words they write are unrecognizable; and the most elementary problems in arithmetic are mysteries to them. No one can deny that the modern school fails to teach the fundamentals to these children.

But these unfortunates are at one end of a wide scale of achievement, and their failure to learn is scanty evidence that today's schools do not teach the fundamentals. Similarly with the child, only a little above the lowest, who misspells the simple words "purpose" and "shower" as "perases" and "shayer," or scrawls the phrase, "to read and wright." This boy or girl may be a miserable speller, but can surely not be cited as the symbol of an untaught generation. The vast majority of children do learn to spell these words correctly, along with others that are even more difficult. Seventy to 90 percent of thirteen-year-olds in good school systems will be able to spell such words as "colonies," "finally," and "citizen." They did so recently when 768 eighth-grade pupils were given a spelling test of fifty words to which no special study had been devoted. When it is considered that the eighth grade of an entire city was tested, including pupils who succeeded on very few words, it is apparent that most of them spelled nearly every word correctly. The 70 to 90 percent of accurate spelling included practically all of the children of normal ability and above. These children *have* learned the fundamentals of spelling. One of them, who can be cited as an example of a pupil at the upper end of the achievement range, scored 100 on every classroom spelling test for three consecutive months.

It is true that many children of meager ability can scarcely learn to distinguish among the tenses of verbs. Often they write such sentences as, "She doesn't like to be call a baby," and, "He was suppose to go." But again, for every one of these students, there is another at the top performance level who wins an essay contest. Hundreds of other pupils are somewhere between in the quality of their language skills.

The differences are just as great in arithmetic. It is no trouble to find the glaring errors of the weakest students. They are the ones who write the lazy, sprawling "2's" and "5's," on their sides as often as not. The seven is three times as large as the one. Their columns of fig-

ures sway back and forth across the page. Addition, subtraction, and the other fundamental operations are little more than guesses. But these are the lowest 2 or 3
percent of the total student body. The only conclusions
their weaknesses can support are limited to their own
efforts. They cannot justify broad generalizations about
all of the teaching in even one class.

WHICH SCHOOLS?

The question, "In which schools?" is also pertinent in
any discussion of the teaching of the fundamentals, although the differences among schools are not as great
as those among individual children. The poorest schools
include some pupils of high ability and motivation who
can and often do learn by their own efforts, just as
most of the schools which rank near the top of the national averages on the standardized tests include some
weak students whose scores are below the average for
any school. Any community of large population will
have in its public-school enrollment an ability range
extensive enough to include both the ablest and the
weakest of students. The range among schools is nar-
rower than among children, but, wholly apart from the
abilities of their individual pupils, schools do vary considerably in the quality of their instruction and learning.

Numerous investigations have shown that the most
important influence in the quality of schools is the level
of their financial support. Money has as much to say in
education as anywhere else in American life. Its presence
in the school's accounts means more and better buildings, equipment, and books for the community's children. Money for higher salaries attracts and holds teach-

ers with more and better training. It can even mean an extra two or three weeks in the school year. All of these have cumulative effects in the education of children. Those who attend the better schools get off to faster starts than their less fortunate contemporaries in other communities, and the differences in achievement increase year by year. Average figures of achievement will show variations among schools of as much as two years by the end of the sixth grade. A brief explanation of the source of these figures will make the comparison clearer.

Most public schools administer standardized achievement tests to all of their pupils at regular intervals. The frequency varies considerably, but the majority of children will be tested at least two or three times during their twelve years of public education. A typical achievement test consists of a "battery" of six or eight individual tests in such common phases of learning as reading speed, reading comprehension, arithmetic, English usage, vocabulary, social studies, and science. The scores furnish a convenient and inexpensive comparison of any pupil's achievement with others' in his own school and in other schools over the country. The scores are "standardized" by giving the tests to several thousand representative children whose average marks provide the standards for comparison among all who take the test subsequently. As a very simple illustration, in which some accuracy has been sacrificed for brevity, suppose that the average score in arithmetic for thousands of sixth-grade pupils is 64. Then any child who attains a score of 64 on this part of the battery, no matter what his actual age or grade may be, has demonstrated sixth-grade ability in arithmetic. A score of 54 indicates less than sixth-grade ability, while a score of

74 shows a higher level of achievement than the sixth grade. Any of these three figures could be the score for a single child, the average for a class, or the average for all of the pupils in a given grade in a city school system.

It sometimes happens, of course, that a child's test scores may change considerably from one testing to another, perhaps from average performance in the sixth grade to above average in the eighth. Or a decline in the youngster's rating may occur. Such a change might happen for several reasons: One of the tests may have been administered carelessly; the child may not have been feeling well on one of the testing days; or the child's attitude toward school may have changed. Cases have been studied in which foster children have made large gains after being moved to superior home environments. Whenever a substantial change in test scores does happen, it is studied by the school's guidance counselors, and the child is re-tested if this seems advisable. The same careful study is made of any cases in which a youngster's test scores are inconsistent with his grades or his teacher's judgment of his abilities.

Although they are seldom cited by the folklorists, scores on the standardized achievement tests are useful measurements of the quality of learning for an individual pupil or for the schools of an entire community. In one school system, for example, average test scores have been in the top 2 to 5 percent of the nation for a number of years. Surely the fundamentals have been taught very well indeed in the modern schools of this city. Just as surely, they have been taught less well in many other modern schools. Test scores do not tell the whole story of education by any means, and they are never used in good schools as the sole evidence upon which decisions about students are made, but this does not impair their usefulness as one source of information about the quality of learning.

The concurrence of lack of ability and lack of opportunity which has been mentioned earlier nearly always results in failure in the learning achievements of the school. These are individual cases which may occur in any normal American community. Even more unfortunate are those collective situations, sometimes involving entire schools, in which children from meager home environments attend schools supported on low financial levels. Here it can only be anticipated that average learnings in the school subjects will be well below achievements under more favorable circumstances elsewhere.

THE LIMITS ON LEARNING ARE REAL

Children's learning of the fundamental subjects cannot be expected to approach uniformity. At least three factors, all of which have been discussed earlier, operate to limit the achievement of every child in every school. They are the child's inherited abilities, the general environment in which he lives, and the quality of the school he attends. Though it may be possible for a particular individual to transcend these limits, perhaps because of unusually strong motivation, such cases are rare. The great majority of children are unable to escape the circumstances which surround them. Hence differences in learning the fundamentals extend over an exceedingly broad range.

Teachers are confronted daily by the reality of the limits upon individual and group learning. Every child in every classroom presents unique instructional problems, because no two have identical combinations of the factors that limit their learning. Usually enough similarities among individuals are present to make group instruction effective, but the differences within a class *can* be so great that the teacher is unable to do all of the individual learning needs full justice. Anyone who listens to the conversations of teachers will hear many descriptions of classes in which these unfavorable conditions are present. He will also become impatient with people who attempt to summarize the teaching of the fundamentals in a single sentence.

To write or speak as though all children could learn to read rapidly with good comprehension, write clearly and interestingly, and figure quickly and accurately if only they had the proper teaching is to encourage false hopes among parents of the less fortunate pupils. Good teaching can increase the achievements of all children, but it cannot take any child beyond his abilities. It is just as misleading to urge that all high-school students take the advanced mathematics and science courses, and to argue that only good teaching is needed for everyone to succeed in these abstract and difficult learnings. But contemporary critics have expressed such untenable views time and again. What they have in effect done is to berate modern education for differences in ability to learn which children bring to the school and which the school can do very little to alter.

SHADES OF TRUTH

The fact is, of course, that almost any conceivable statement about the teaching of the fundamentals contains some shade of truth, for at least a few children can be found for whom it is an accurate description. But no single statement can be true for any very large segment of the pupil population of the public schools unless it has been qualified by recognition of the conditions under which the schools operate. More accuracy can be added by specific references to certain, identifiable children in definite schools. If a true understanding of the teaching of the fundamentals is sought, the performances of many children in many situations must be analyzed. This is exactly the opposite of the methods by which the conclusions of folklore are reached.

Even though the folk belief of children's failure to learn the fundamentals in modern schools is slightly tinged with truth, this is but feeble justification for the sweeping statements that lump together all pupils in all schools. Statements of this sort are never true for more than a small percentage of children, and they vary from partially to completely false for all of the others. The basic inaccuracy of this scrap of educational folklore should have removed it from serious consideration long ago. The analysis of the achievements of many children will show that most of them do learn the fundamentals reasonably well. A small percentage scarcely learn them at all, but an equal or perhaps slightly larger number become nearly perfect in the elementary branches of learning which comprise the fundamentals.

THE TIMELESS QUOTATION

The complaint that the schools no longer teach as well as they once did surely is one of the most ancient of mythologies. It is, indeed, a well-worn and timeless comment, often repeated by a few of the elders of every age. Americans were saying it fifty years ago of the schools of which today's folklorists speak so proudly. It was being said a hundred years ago also. Such is the indestructibility of the myth that it may well endure another half-century—to the ultimate glorification of the schools of the 1960's. Imagine a middle-aged college professor in the year 2000 complaining that the public schools do not teach the fundamentals as well as they did in 1960 when he was a child!

The writings of the ancient Greeks, who seem to have had words for everything, included comments on the deterioration of the education of their youth. Then as now, critics looked back to the schools of their childhood when all things were better. If these portions of the record of history were to be taken seriously, it would mean that the teaching of the fundamentals has been going downhill for at least twenty-five hundred years.

Who has not read at least one excerpt from an essay or speech lamenting the quality of modern education, only to discover from a footnote that it had been said long ago in other times? Such statements make interesting fillers for magazines, and many of them have been published in recent years. Along with Mom's cooking, yesterday's schools remain among the most favorable of men's memories. They are the schools of thirty years ago for one writer. Another prefers the teaching of 1910, and a third likes the schools of the nineteenth century. Whatever their time, they belong to the glorious days in which *everyone* was taught to read, write, spell, and cipher perfectly.

THE ADULT-TO-CHILD RELATIONSHIP CAN BE DECEIVING

Complaints about neglect of the fundamentals are often reinforced by descriptions of the lack of knowledge and skills among children with whom the narrator is acquainted. Opening with remarks about learning the critic says, "They can't do this . . . ," and "They can't do that . . . ," and continues with a personal reference such as "Now when I was their age. . . ." The modern child seldom comes out even with his elders in these comparisons. The account of his achievements is not flattering, nor is it intended to be, for he is cast as the darkened foil before whom the image of the young scholar of folklore is to shine. The luster of this image undoubtedly appears more convincing because it is being invoked by an adult, whose experience in the matter a youngster can do little but accept as authoritative.

The position of the adult in contacts with children is, indeed, a frequent source of self-deception. The advantages of grown men and women in both education and experience over the youngsters in their own social circles are always considerable. Most adults also enjoy some measures of economic and social power which are still years away from the children, but to which all but the youngest have learned to pay some deference. Unless the older person can learn to view the relationship as one in which maturity confronts only partial development, his constant superiority will mislead him into underestimating the ability and learning of his junior. Better understanding results when the adult can bring himself to visualize the man the boy is on his way to becoming, as well as what he is at present.

Teachers must also be on guard against the same temptation to feel superior to the children in their classes. Anyone who has taught any of the public school subjects a number of times should be able to solve its most difficult problems with ease. His capabilities are far beyond the present achievements of all except the most brilliant students, since the children are experiencing the subject for the first time. The teacher's feelings of superiority are moderated, however, by the knowledge that at least some of his pupils will go on to surpass his own best performances.

The adult's position on the upper end of the maturity-immaturity relationship with children can easily lead him to overlook the child's growing processes, and cause him to regard the temporary differences between him and the children as something permanent. When this happens, there is danger that the adult may really come to believe that children today are simply not learning as well as he once did. And since the adult continues to have the same kind of experiences, he may never have occasion to doubt his conclusion, each new observation seeming in fact further to confirm it.

THOSE BRIGHT GRANDDADS

Middle-aged teachers whom enlightened communities have permitted to spend their careers in one school system, occasionally meet in their classes the slow-learning children of parents they met as slow learners a generation ago. Mamma and Daddy had about the same difficulties in learning the fundamentals then, as their children have today. But most of them left the school much earlier in life. Society has become more solicitous about providing educational opportunities for all youngsters, and today's children attend school for more years than their parents did. Teaching careers seldom span enough years for the children's teachers to have taught the grandparents also, but it is reasonable to assume that some of them were slow learners too. This does not mean, of course, that the characteristics of slow learning are inescapable family traits, but they do appear frequently in successive generations.

The possibility of slow learners in the schools of two generations ago has no place in the folklore of education which has fashioned an image of grandparents who learned the fundamentals thoroughly. They were the pupils in the fine schools in which the teachers really taught subjects. The vision of such an instructor's paradise, in which all children learned so readily, should make today's teachers feel they were born too late. What pleasure teaching must have been when all of those bright granddads were children!

THE SCHOOLS DO MORE FOR THE SLOW LEARNERS NOW

Since nearly all children now attend school for more years than ever before, the less bright ones may be remembered more clearly by the elders of the future. Certainly they are too prominent in today's schools to be overlooked by anyone who has even the slightest first-hand acquaintance with the current problems of education. Whether they are scattered through the regular classes or grouped together for special instruction, their presence is evident at all times. However, their situations are more hopeful today than formerly. More is known about their learning problems as well as about their needs for special attention.

Where there is provision for small classes in which specially trained teachers adapt lessons to the ages and abilities of the children, the slower students often make progress which, for them, is truly remarkable. This necessitates, of course, that the irrational folklore of uniform children and subjects be replaced by accurate diagnosis of each child's learning problems and careful matching of assignments to individual abilities. Slow-learning students in the eighth grade, for example, work on materials at whatever level (and assuming, of course, reasonable expenditures of time and energy) are discovered to be manageable *for them*. They are encouraged and allowed to progress as rapidly as they are able, without regard for the conventional timetable of one grade per year.

Near the lowest extreme of achievement among children in the eighth grade are some whose best performances are on third- and fourth-grade levels of achievement. This has been their accomplishment in seven or more years of school. Most of them have spent more than one year in at least one grade and are well past the normal eighth-grade age of thirteen. In many cases, good teaching has enabled these children to increase subject achievement as much as two years within a single year of school. In one instance, a fourth-grade level of achievement at the beginning of the year was raised to sixth-grade performance before the end. Another child increased her achievement from fifth- to seventh-grade level. Neither of these is at all exceptional, for in some classes of this sort nearly every child does as well. They still remain well below normal eighth-grade achievement, but they are getting the sort of education their known learning needs require. The same thing, naturally, can happen in the fifth or sixth, or any other grade. Although the eighth grade has been chosen for this illustration, instances of effective remedial teaching can be supplied for other grades also. This does not mean that all slow-learning children can do as well, for some can hardly be helped by the best of teaching, but excellent individual records of progress have been made in arithmetic, in reading, in the social studies, and in science.

Perhaps some critics of the public schools will be alarmed that children of thirteen or older are studying lessons which were designed for ten-year-olds. Does this not prove neglect of the fundamentals? But these special classes include only a very small fraction of the children of their age groups, usually no more than 2 or 3 percent. Nothing from the folklore of education can meet their educational needs. They cannot succeed at the learning tasks which are normal for their ages. This has been demonstrated over and over in every year they have attended school. As for increasing the severity of discipline, most of them have already received far more than their share of punishment. It is worthy of note that their work habits and their attitudes toward school and teachers usually improve as they begin to make progress. And occasionally a few of these children accomplish so much that they can be placed in the normal classes for their grades. This is not neglect of learning. The children benefit from extremely effective teaching of the fundamentals by means of skillful adaptations to individually diagnosed learning difficulties. Nor are their learning problems solved at the expense of brighter, more educable children, as one of the persistent myths of education would have it. The same general procedures of diagnosis and adaptation are just as effective with the brighter majority as with the slow learners, although the specific materials and methods of teaching are quite different.

MORE FUNDAMENTALS FOR ALL

Improvements in the teaching of the fundamental subjects to slow learners are typical of general increases in effectiveness in the instruction of all children. The discipline of education has advanced with the other disciplines, although its progress has not been highlighted by achievements as dramatic as the spectacular accomplishments of aeronautics, electronics, and nuclear fission. It seems to be in the nature of the public's attitudes toward the schools that their unfortunate incidents make news while their steady but quiet progress receives little notice.

The learnings of youth in the secondary schools are useful in contrasting the efficiency of the teaching of different periods, for they are based upon the fundamental knowledges and skills of the elementary school. Yet comparisons of pupil achievements across the generations are misleading unless they match students of approximately the same abilities. The student populations of modern high schools include large numbers of average and below-average youth. The selective high schools of 1890 and 1900 retained very few students of these levels of ability. No one should expect the average achievement of the more than 70 percent of American youth who now attend high school to equal the learnings of the 7 percent who were enrolled in 1890. If a comparison of the academic achievements of the two periods is desired, the upper 10 percent of today's student body should be contrasted with all of the students of the earlier high school. Most of today's selected youth will not be able to match their predecessors' learnings in Latin, Greek, and ancient history, for the trend has been strongly away from the study of these subjects, but their accomplishments in science, mathematics, English, American history, and the modern foreign languages will more than compensate.

Interesting evidence of greater efficiency in modern schools appears in the intensified competition among high-school graduates for admission to the colleges they consider most desirable. Students have very definite preferences among institutions of higher education, and they highly prize admission to those of their first choice. The same scores on college entrance examinations which would have enabled graduates to choose among colleges a few years ago would rank only a little above the average today. The fact that admission to college is more difficult to attain than ever before is no evidence of the superiority of modern schools, of course. The better known colleges and universities now have many times the number of applicants they can accommodate. But the substantial increases in the test scores of high-school juniors and seniors are undeniable proof of the effectiveness of their teaching in modern public schools. And these increases have been made in the same recent years in which the critics have claimed to see a serious deterioration in secondary education.

BETTER TEACHING AND BETTER FACILITIES

The general rise in student achievement is clearly attributable to better teaching and better facilities. In the last three or four decades, teaching has moved rapidly toward professionalization. Teachers now know more about teaching and about their subjects than ever before. Every state now requires for teacher certification college preparation in both the subjects to be taught and the professional courses in education. Only a generation ago, it was possible to teach in many states with little or no education on the college level in either the school subjects or the methods of teaching. And while in the current teacher shortage some thousands of ill-prepared teachers do serve with emergency certificates, they comprise only a small minority of public-school teachers. For the profession as a whole, the long term trend has been toward more and better preparation. (There is no intent here to overlook the harsh criticisms which have been directed at the professional courses in education. They will receive full consideration in Chapter XIII.)

Both the quality and the volume of teaching aids have also increased greatly. Resources available to teachers only twenty-five years ago were meager in comparison with those which are readily obtainable today. Textbooks have changed tremendously. Not only are they more attractive, but they have been written specifically to meet the needs of the children who use them. No longer is it necessary for pupils to study a reworked college text which confronts them with vocabulary and sentence structure several years beyond their abilities. Thousands of films and film strips bring the world into the classroom. Colorful charts have been developed for use in the sciences and social studies. And the libraries of good schools are full of books on every pertinent topic. Moreover, the children of this generation are taught the skills of using library resources. They learn to use reference materials by consulting them to complete their class projects and assignments.

The range of individual achievement remains as great as ever, for children cannot often escape the limits which life has placed upon their abilities to learn, but improvements have been effected all along the line. More children now learn more fundamentals than ever before. Slow learners remain in school longer, and they achieve more. Those in the normal ranges of ability also do better. And those fortunate ones who are blessed with both high ability and excellent opportutunity enjoy the most favorable situations of all. Their happy circumstances are of such scope that they merit the separate treatment they are to receive in the next chapter.

10. The Happy Plight of the Gifted Child

To the exceptionally bright and industrious children fall the most auspicious educational opportunities of all. Never before have their opportunities been so great and their rewards so lavish as in the contemporary American public schools. Modern techniques insure their early identification, and modern educational programs serve their learning needs. Higher education promises liberal financial aid when they have completed secondary school.

THE MELANCHOLY FOLKLORE

In the folklore of education, it is fashionable just now to speak in gloomy tones of the plight of the "gifted child." He is declared to be the neglected one in the public school systems of our country. Alarm is expressed lest his interests be sacrificed to the needs of the slower students who are said to receive more than their share of the teachers' time and efforts. According to this view, the bright children are left to guide themselves through the curriculum with little or no assistance from the school.

It may be that the present wave of concern for these gifted children will bring them even greater opportunities and rewards than have already been provided for them. If this is so, it will be all to the good. Yet the fact must be emphasized that they have by no means been neglected. Some of the chief aspects of their already favorable situation are described in the remaining sections of this chapter.

EARLY IDENTIFICATION

A number of modern techniques now enable teachers to ascertain the brightness of children at an early age. Standardized tests in common use include those designed to measure intelligence, reading, subject achievement, and aptitudes. Each of the tests yields a score which compares each child with thousands of others on the same grade level. Those whose scores are consistently high are easily spotted. These children are not overlooked in the classroom. They do not "blush unseen." They soon become known and watched throughout the school. The standardized tests alone guarantee the early discovery of the bright child.

The individual folder is another technique widely used in modern schools. Here is assembled the child's cumulative record for his entire public school career—test scores, anecdotes of behavior, grades, teachers' judgments of ability, and the health record are all included. The folder for each child contains the history of his education. The most cursory inspection can reveal the true measure of his ability and industriousness, but such records are examined regularly and systematically by specialists who have been trained in their use.

Because of their personal nature, guidance folders are protected as confidential material. They are never opened for public inspection, nor for any other casual purpose. Only qualified, professional personnel are permitted to see them. Both common sense and professional ethics make such protective policies necessary, but within the school the guidance folders are available to teachers and guidance specialists at all times.

With respect to identification, the talented child receives the same treatment as everyone else. But the point here made, which is so often ignored, is that this identification is early, definite, and unmistakable.

The most capable children are expected to do more than those of ordinary ability. Because teachers are just as human as anyone else, notwithstanding the slurs of folklore, they take considerable pride in the quality of their students' work. Everyone enjoys success and recognition, and so do teachers. They like to show the excellence of the work which has been done in their classes, the work turned out by the best students. Teachers are quick to notice any decline in the bright child's efforts, but this does not often happen among the really bright. Few of the best students need much prodding; with a little imagination and stimulation from adults they perform consistently at high levels of achievement, thereby delighting their teachers and stimulating themselves to more of the same kind of performance.

ABILITY AND INDUSTRIOUSNESS MARK THE TOP STUDENT

Ability merely gives a child the *potential* for serious achievement. To realize the potential, ability must be combined with sufficient industry to complete difficult and extended learning tasks. Brightness alone, though noticed in the classroom, has little value unless it is accompanied by seriousness of purpose. The child with the high IQ, who will not work, is known to every teacher. Probably the number, if not the ability, of such children is somewhat exaggerated because they are mentioned so frequently, but they are present in every school.

Industrious, but less bright, children, are also identified. They are welcomed in every classroom, because teachers admire their diligent attitudes, but they seldom become the top-ranking students. They perform reasonably well on most assignments, but only dimly glimpse the more abstract points of the subject materials.

Ability and industriousness occur in every conceivable combination, and so contribute to the great range of achievement among individual children. No one can remain near the top of the range unless he possesses a high degree of both. It is quite probable, moreover, that ability unaccompanied by industry eventually deteriorates into mediocrity.

Many educators have learned to avoid the use of the word "gifted" when referring to the specially talented children. For one thing, it is an emotional term, making objectivity difficult. For another, "gifted" is a vague word connoting many vague possibilities. Individuals have many different kinds of gifts, some of which have no relation to school work, though they may be of great value to the person and to his society. Hence the tendency to avoid the term and use more descriptive phrases such as "students with ability and industry." A number of such phrases are in use among educators, all of them improvements upon the single word "gifted." There can be no misunderstanding when one speaks of students who have ability and industriousness.

THE FORTUNATE ARE FEW

There are very few truly bright and highly motivated students in any unclassified school population—many fewer than parents imagine. Occasionally, however, a high concentration of such students is found within one school. The school system of a metropolis can select the top two or three percent of students for their ability, interest, and industry, and put all of them in one specialized high school where nearly all will do excellent work. Such happy circumstances are comparatively rare, but they are so well publicized that they seem to be a common occurrence. They furnish ammunition for the casual critic who denounces the local high school for not maintaining the same uniform standards of learning as the highly selective institution whose program he has just seen described on his television screen. But only a few cities are large enough to organize selective high schools of this type. In the great majority of American communities all the local youth attend one secondary school, which must provide for all levels of ability and all kinds of purposes. This need not mean that the brightest students are neglected; there are many possibilities for exploiting their brightness. But it is nonsense for anyone to expect 1,500 unselected students to perform on the same academic level as 1,500 who represent the top two percent of the total number from which they were chosen.

PANELS AND PROGRAMS

There are innumerable opportunities for enriching the education of the able and industrious student. Among the first to be encountered by the child is the practice of performing before groups of other persons. This begins in the early years of the elementary school and continues through the twelfth grade, gaining in both scope and intensity as the maturity of the pupils increases. Even in the first grade, children appear in simple programs and pageants before parent audiences and elementary school assemblies. Panel discussions, in which several pupils present their views on a chosen topic to the rest of the class, also begin in the elementary school. The best students, of course, play the feature roles most frequently. Only the naïve would expect the teacher-directors to rely upon any except the most able to carry the most responsible parts in performances which are attended by principals, supervisors, and parents. Less talented children are not omitted from the productions. Usually they are assigned minor roles or stage duties.

Opportunities in the secondary schools are even more numerous and more demanding. Students in these age groups are more capable of performing before critical audiences than the younger children. They are able to sustain a presentation of longer duration and greater complexity, whether it be a panel, a pageant, or a play.

Most of these public experiences are of educational value to the students who participate in them. Useful learnings are acquired when children study a topic intensively and develop their findings for a panel discussion. Entertainment programs are somewhat less valuable as learning experiences, since they seldom require children to study any subject matter, but they do contribute to music and speech education, and often they are extremely helpful in the formation of desirable personality traits.

Certain types of performances, especially those in music and athletics, may require different kinds of abilities which may not be possessed by the brightest students. On the whole, however, there can be no doubt that these activities also feature the most able children and youth in the school. For, in general, these tend to include the best musicians and athletes who can be found or developed in the student body.

SCIENCE FAIRS

Each year thousands upon thousands of junior and senior high school students prepare projects for exhibition in Science Fairs. Regional or county winners in the several classes proceed to state-level competition, and a few go on to try for national honors. Interest has grown rapidly in this fairly recent innovation. Hundreds of exhibits may be seen in the Science Fair for a single populous county, and each year more than a quarter of a million youngsters exhibit their projects somewhere in the country.

The quality of most of the entries in a Science Fair is excellent. Perhaps the current criticism of the public schools would be less bitter if the critics would take half a day to browse through one of these fine exhibitions. Many of the student scientists have used a large proportion of their free time for months, spending hundreds of hours in the preparation of their projects. Often a youth has combined learnings from two or more courses, perhaps mathematics and physics, to complete his project. Very likely his search for information has necessitated reading extensively beyond the subject matter of his high-school courses. He may have visited a university campus or a research laboratory to confer with a specialist in the field of his project. Other entrants have concentrated on the construction of their projects. Some, for example, have machined metal parts wholly by themselves and to their own original designs.

Almost any type of scientific project one could name is likely to be among the exhibits in a Science Fair. The variety of projects is endless. If the real thing is beyond a student's means, he constructs a model of it. The fields of bacteria, plant experiments, rockets, satellites, conservation, electronics, weather, pressure and temperature, sound, aeronautics, fuel, mechanics, and many others are represented. The ingenuity of American youth is inexhaustibly fertile in this respect, as in others.

Can anyone who has seen a Science Fair doubt that he has observed the work of the brightest students? As a learning opportunity, this is "tailor made" for the youngsters who possess large amounts of both ability and industry.

RECOGNITION OF ACHIEVEMENT

Programs and Science Fairs are splendid opportunities for bright children to utilize their abilities, but they are by no means their only avenues to recognition. Other chances to gain public notice are offered in every school. One of the most common is the Honor Roll, which lists the names of the students of high scholastic standing a distinction which some earn year after year.

Additional opportunities are presented in the secondary school honor societies. These are usually national in scope, with chapters in local high schools. Because they are most common in the larger schools, membership is not available to the students of many small high schools. However, the great majority of American youth attend city high schools where there are almost certain to be honor societies. The largest and best known of these distinctive groups is the National Honor Society, with well over 4,000 chapters, whose more than 200,000 members by 1959-60 were chosen for their qualities of scholarship, character, leadership, and service to the school. Other national societies recognize more specific achievements on the same high level of quality. Masque and Gavel honors students for excellence in speech and dramatics. Membership in Quill and Scroll signifies outstanding performance in high-school journalism. As its name implies, the French National Honor Society confers recognition for superior accomplishment in that language.

Recognition for any student is motivation for others. Whenever performances of high quality are honored in the school, other students are inspired to seek the same distinction. Undoubtedly, thousands of high school freshmen, sophomores, and juniors, who have seen the senior awards conferred, have resolved to themselves, "I'll be up there when I'm a senior." The attention which is given to outstanding academic performances serves the double purpose of recognizing superiority and stimulating ambition in younger students.

ACCELERATION IN THE ADVANCED PLACEMENT PROGRAM

The completely departmentalized program of the senior high school offers more possibilities for varying

the schedules of individual students than the undiffer-
entiated class schedules of the elementary and junior
high schools, in which pupils spend most or all of the
day in the same groups. A great variety of elective subjects adds to the possibilities. With a few exceptions the
assignment of students to classes for any period in the
day is entirely independent of the assignment for any
other period. Since departmentalization was described
in Chapter VIII, it is necessary only to mention the
favorable situation which is created for selective teaching of any group of students, including those of highest
potential.

In nearly nine hundred high schools throughout the
country, classes of exceptional students are regularly
organized in the Advanced Placement Program to cover
more than the prescribed amounts of subject matter.
According to an article in the New York *Times* on
October 30, 1960, 10,531 students from 890 high schools
took in 1959 the College Entrance Examination Board's
tests for courses of college level studied in high school.

The members of advanced placement classes are selected after careful scrutiny of their school records with
regard to such factors as level of ability, achievement,
grades, and teachers' recommendations. Since each class
can be organized independently of any other, a high
degree of selectivity is possible. A group which has
been organized as a class in mathematics need have no
connection with other classes in mathematics or in any
other subject, since it exists as a group only during the
daily period for which it has been scheduled.

Eleventh-grade mathematics will furnish a good illustration. Suppose that 125 students who have passed
tenth-grade plane geometry have chosen mathematics
as one of their subjects for the next year. Nearly all are

far above the average in mathematics. Selective factors
of interest, industry, and ability have eliminated many
others who began the study of elementary algebra with
these students in the ninth grade, and earlier divisions
by ability and interest had been made before ninth
grade mathematics. Most high-school principals would
arrange five sections of the eleventh grade course to accommodate these 125 students, and they could, if they
wished, exercise careful choice in assigning individuals
to sections.

Under these circumstances, to be found in all large,
comprehensive high schools, it is easily possible to select
the twenty-five most promising mathematics students
for an accelerated section. They are not selected for
general ability on the basis of an IQ alone, but on the
record of their specific, demonstrated abilities in
mathematics. This is far from the uncritical use of the
IQ with which some critics have charged the schools.

Such a class has tremendous potentials. These students are exceedingly quick to learn, they are superior
in resourcefulness, and they have developed excellent
work habits. Their capabilities should enable them to
complete two semesters' work in one with relative ease.
For example, solid geometry and trigonometry usually
require one semester each in high school, but a class
selected in the manner described above has been known
to complete both in twelve weeks of class time.

Students in these highly selected classes can easily do
four years of mathematics in their three years in the
senior high school. This means that they can be ready
in the twelfth grade to take the courses designed for
college freshmen. By passing advanced placement examinations over these courses they can earn advanced

standing in college mathematics, entitling them to enter sophomore courses in their first year.

The procedures of selection and acceleration, much the same in the other academic subjects of English, social studies, foreign languages, and science, are used today in the best high schools all over the country. The percentage of students is small, to be sure, but the number is rather large, and it is increasing rapidly. In 1959 more than 10,000 high school seniors took college level courses in which they used college textbooks and wrote college examinations.

By the time he is a senior, the bright and industrious student has thus had abundant opportunities for recognition, honor, and stimulation. But the best rewards are still to come. As he looks ahead to further education, he finds the colleges seeking him out with generous offers of scholarships.

SCHOLARSHIPS ARE LARGE AND NUMEROUS

The total value of the scholarships awarded to the members of a single class of seniors in a large American high school sometimes amounts to more than $100,000. The individual awards vary from less than one hundred dollars to a sum large enough to pay for all four years of college. While some high schools have been able to do more for their graduates than others in preparing them for these rich awards, any student anywhere who has shown high scholastic achievement is eligible for many attractive scholarships.

Moreover, both the number and the value of college scholarships are increasing rapidly. A listing and description of the total number of scholarships now available to high school graduates would fill an entire book. Indeed, books which do just this have been published for the guidance of teachers, students, and parents. The United States Office of Education issued in 1951 a bulletin entitled, "Scholarships and Fellowships Available at Institutions of Higher Education." Another bulletin from the same office in 1957 was "Financial Aid for College Students." S. Norman Feingold's three volumes, *Scholarships, Fellowships, and Loans,* Bellman Publishing Co., appeared in 1949, 1951, and 1955.

Both the cash value and the prestige of the scholarship confer honor upon the recipient, for whom this is the pinnacle of a long sequence of recognitions and rewards in the public schools. Those who have excelled in ability and industry have enjoyed a gratifying prominence from their early years in the elementary school to the final pageant at which they receive their high-school diplomas.

AND SOON SUBSIDIES?

The next step to aid children and youth with superior intellectual ability may be a broad financial assistance program at public expense to enable needy students to complete high school. Educators have known for many years that the state of family finances has prevented many high ranking high-school graduates from attending college and has caused others to leave high school before graduation. These conditions, which were presented more fully in Chapter VII, have lately become known to others, who, perhaps because of their prominence, have been able to attract more attention to the situation, so that it is now a familiar topic in discussions of public education.

To permit students of high ability to leave school prematurely is a waste of human resources. The basic principles of conservation are appropriate here as in any situation where precious resources are under consideration. But unlike some other national reserves which can remain underground until needed, human abilities cannot wait. The early drop-outs soon acquire responsibilities which will prevent most of them from ever returning.

No other public investment earns as much on its principal as the money which is invested in education. This is as true for the nation as for the individual who profits from his education. The increase in ability to pay taxes, even if no other benefits were received, would more than repay the public investment needed to enable more youth of high ability to become technicians, scientists, and professional practitioners.

It now seems probable that the first efforts to give financial assistance to needy youth will soon be made. Some sort of public, tax-supported program may be anticipated, but support from private means may also be provided, for here is an opportunity for one of the large foundations to take the lead in an educational program of the highest merit. It would be feasible, for example, for some scholarships to begin while students are still in the high school, instead of waiting until their entrance to college. Surely it makes more sense to give help at the stage where it is most needed than to offer it arbitrarily only at the college level.

WHO IS NEGLECTED?

The typical bright child, who is also industrious, has been identified early in his school career. He, or she, has been featured in innumerable programs of all sorts, some before groups of classmates and others for adult audiences. If he is so inclined, he has prepared and exhibited science projects in competition with other students of high ability. Most of his teachers have worked hard to stimulate him to reach the limits of his ability. His name has been listed regularly on the school's Honor Roll. Not as typically, but with increasing frequency, he has taken at least one accelerated course for which he will receive advanced placement in college. He has been accepted into the membership of one or more of the high-school societies which honor high achievement. He leaves the public school with a generous college scholarship. In nearly every high school of large enrollment each graduating class boasts several students who have earned every one of these impressive honors.

Perhaps there are public schools somewhere in which bright children are neglected. But the *opportunities* for success which have been described in this chapter are to be found everywhere. All of them are of national scope, well publicized, and participated in by thousands of students. Were they not available in the schools of a given community, surely parents who had learned of them elsewhere would insist that such opportunities be offered to their own children.

As in so many other cases, the facts of the school program have been characteristically ignored by those who complain that, "They don't do enough for the gifted." The folk belief of "neglected ability" dissolves into myth when real programs in real schools are examined. In fact, the most able and industrious students are recognized, stimulated, and rewarded throughout their careers in the public schools.

But the truly bright comprise only a small percentage of the millions of children who go to school. Earlier chapters have included brief descriptions of the differentiated programs by which the educational needs of all are served. Contemplation of the variety brings up an important question: Is not the very scope of these offerings a threat to the intellectual purposes for which the public schools were founded? So much has been said about nonintellectualism in modern education that the topic is examined in some detail in the chapter which follows.

11. The Legend of Anti-intellectualism

A recent addition to the folklore of American education is the charge that the schools have become anti-intellectual. Perhaps because "anti-intellectual" has an enticing polysyllabic ring, or perhaps because it provides a convenient label for those who wish to indulge in blanket condemnation, the accusation of anti-intellecutalism is well on its way to becoming a stubbornly resistent modern myth.

THE HIGH SCHOOL UNDER FIRE

The favorite target for the accusation of anti-intellectualism has been the American public high school. It has been criticized severely and repeatedly for both the quality of instruction and its program of subjects. Quality has been attacked on the grounds that American youngsters are not made to work as hard as their parents and grandparents. The high-school program has been under heavy fire because students are not required to take its most difficult subjects.

These accusations invariably appear in a context rich with the folklore of education. The reverie of an earlier Golden Age, the fantasy of a single standard for all, and the myth of the uniform student are all prominent. Since we have considered these folk beliefs in detail in the earlier chapters of this book, it seems unnecessary to do more than identify them here as folklore. But let us examine the charges against quality and program more closely, confining our argument to the secondary school—the main target for this criticism.

"WHICH STUDENTS?" IS PERTINENT

Critics must face up to the fundamental question of *which students* lack good instruction and therefore the energy to study and learn. As in all other known aspects of human behavior, enormous differences occur in students' work output. But there has never been a real shortage of serious students in American high schools. These students are the youngsters who complete all of their assignments accurately and regularly, who work for extra credit at every opportunity, and who rank near the top in their examinations. They are numerous and very much in evidence. Now that more incentives are being offered to students of high academic achievement than ever before, the percentage of truly serious students is on the increase.

The nation's current needs for more technicians and professional workers of every sort have also had favorable effects on the work attitudes of capable high-school students, for they have realized the urgency of the international situation as readily as adults. Records of the ways in which out-of-school time is used show large numbers of junior and senior high-school students doing many hours of homework each week. Many others, of course, spend little or no time on homework. Neither group offers a reliable basis for any generalization about all high-school students. The true picture is that of a wide range of individuals, who among them exhibit every conceivable degree of effort.

WHO TAKES THE DIFFICULT SUBJECTS?

The foundations of technical and professional education are laid in the high-school years. Here are developed the general abilities of written and oral expression, speed and comprehension in reading, the capacity for self-direction, and efficient work habits. Here also are available the courses in science and mathematics which are preliminary to technical and professional education on the university level. Much of the current criticism of anti-intellectualism has centered about the number of high-school students who take these subjects.

The senior high school differs markedly from the elementary and junior high schools in offering its students opportunities to choose among a variety of subjects. From the kindergarten through the ninth grade, at which point students leave the junior high school, all students take substantially the same program of subjects, with such obvious exceptions as separating the girls and boys for homemaking and shop and for physical education. Elective subjects ordinarily appear for the first time in the ninth grade, but the student usually has no more than one choice, since his program consists chiefly of required subjects. The senior high school offers much more choice. Half or even more of the student's courses may be elective. The senior high school exercises the function of *differentiation* among students to a much greater extent than the earlier schools. Because of the number and diversity of subject offerings, a large American high school is really many schools within a school.

In choosing their elective subjects high-school students are aided by the advice of trained and experienced counselors. Individual abilities, purposes, and previous school records are important considerations in guiding each student in his choice of the courses that are best for him. College entrance requirements are considered in the planning for all who intend to continue their formal education beyond high school. Often the counselors suggest college to capable students who have not considered it before. Educational counseling is taken seriously in high schools everywhere. Rarely will any student be allowed to take courses very much above or below his demonstrated ability without being made aware of the inappropriateness of his choice.

Ability and purpose are selective factors which separate students into groups by influencing their choice of subjects. The high-school courses in physics and chemistry, for example, are highly selective because of their difficulty. No useful purpose is served by putting them on the schedules of students who could have no hope of succeeding in them, and such assignments could do serious harm to the attitudes and work habits of youngsters as they experienced daily frustrations in tasks beyond their capacities. The senior high-school courses in mathematics are similar in their selective effects. Most high-school students, having learned a good deal about the difficulty of the various subjects, are quite realistic in fitting their choices of courses to their abilities, even without the advice of the counselors.

Recently a number of critical commentators have maintained that every student should take all of the mathematics and science courses the high school offers. This must mean that they believe all students have the abilities to succeed in these subjects. But this is the myth of the uniform student all over again. It is quite probable that the present enrollments in these courses reflect student abilities rather accurately. The most recent available figures of high-school science enrollment, those for the school year of 1958-59, show that about 21 percent were taking biology, 8 percent were taking chemistry, and 5 percent were taking physics. But these figures are misleading, unless one takes into account that biology is a course taken almost exclusively by tenth graders, chemistry by eleventh graders, and physics by twelfth graders. Probably these numbers include most of the students who could profit from taking the courses. Undoubtedly, a major cause of the grade-by-grade decline in science enrollments is the increasing difficulty of the subjects. Even if large numbers of other students were required to take chemistry and physics, as some critics of the public high school seem to desire, the quality of their learning could hardly be of value either to themselves or to the advancement of science. Any demand for technical services of the "D" students in science must surely be very limited. Nor is it a contribution to intellectualism to insist that young people take courses that are beyond their capacities.

Enrollments in high-school mathematics courses exhibit much the same trends as in science. At this time, about two-thirds of high-school graduates have taken elementary algebra, about two-fifths have taken plane geometry, and about one-third have taken intermediate algebra. In either science or mathematics, each advanced course may be expected to be more selective and have a smaller enrollment.

Individual interests further increase the selectivity of the advanced high-school courses as students divide to follow the sequences of the different curricula. Because of the specialization of interests in the last two years of the high school, no junior or senior elective course can be expected to attract a majority of the students. Those who have chosen the commercial curriculum, for example, seldom take chemistry or physics, just as the students in the college preparatory curriculum rarely choose to take a course in shorthand. In addition to the required subjects, taken by all students, each curriculum offers a different sequence of elective courses. Each sequence has value for those whose abilities and purposes are best served by it, but no single sequence can meet everybody's educational needs.

INTELLECTUAL FOR MANY

The intellectuality of the American high school varies according to the abilities and interests of its students. For many students, secondary education is a highly intellectual experience in which they study and learn tremendous amounts of difficult, abstract material. Courses in English, history, foreign languages, science, and mathematics crowd the schedules of these students. Often they take five academic subjects instead of the normal load of four. It is not at all unusual for an able student to complete three years each of English, mathematics, science, and history and two or three years of language in his three years in the senior high school. For such students the high school is truly intellectual.

And surely the same must be said for the elementary and junior high schools which they attended and in which they acquired the fundamental learnings. The education of these students has been intellectual at every step, and it will continue to be so in the colleges of their choice.

LESS INTELLECTUAL FOR OTHERS

Because the programs of the public schools must encompass the educational needs of *all* children and youth, experiences for some are lower in intellectual quality. No school can be more intellectual than the abilities and interests of its students, but since so much variation occurs in both of these attributes, great diversities are also present in the intellectualism within a single school. (This also happens in colleges.) Many courses, the required American history for example, can be taught and learned on any number of different levels of difficulty. Just as some senior high-school youngsters learn less history than some pupils in junior high schools, so others actually learn more than some students in colleges. This is not a phenomenon peculiar to modern high schools. Similar spreads in learning have always occurred in schools with large enrollments of unselected students.

Large numbers of students in today's high schools choose curricula other than the college preparatory. Among the most popular of these are the commercial and vocational curricula. (Refer to the chart on page 160 for examples of these curricula.) Students who enroll in them take the general subjects required of everyone for graduation, typically including three years of English, two years of history, a year of mathematics, and two years of science in the four-year span from the ninth through the twelfth grades. The rest of their courses are taken in the areas in which these students specialize. Admittedly, these courses are less intellectual than the chemistry, physics, advanced mathematics, and foreign languages of the college preparatory curriculum. However, they are as intellectual as is appropriate to the abilities and purposes of these students. Although more emphasis is placed upon things practical, such as typing, intellectualism in its proper meaning of "knowing" is always present.

ANTI-INTELLECTUAL FOR NONE

No high schools today exhibit anything of the hostility to knowing which is implied by the term, *anti-intellectualism*. The topic is not under debate in the public schools, for no one there speaks against the intellectual processes of reasoning and understanding. It is safe to say that every professionally educated adult who works in an American public school would like to see *more* reasoning and *more* understanding by students. But all of them also know from their own experiences that these are possible only within the limits of individual circumstances.

Variations in intellectualism in the public high schools are of two kinds. One is the substitution, for students for whom they are suited, of less abstract courses for the traditional college preparatory subjects. The other kind of variation happens because of differences in abilities and interests among the students who are enrolled in any given subject. The introduction of new courses is always intentional, but variations in individual performances occur whether or not anyone has planned for them. They are better learning experiences when they have been planned to match students' capacities than when they represent varying degrees of failure to achieve inflexible objectives. Neither kind of variation signifies a trend *against* intellectualism. Both the new courses and the modifications to serve individual differences represent intelligent efforts to match courses and students for the best interests of both. This is now done fairly well in a great many high schools. It will be done better in the future as more is learned from experience and communicated throughout the profession. At the present time as much intellectualism as students can use is available to them in most American high schools.

NONINTELLECTUAL AT TIMES

The activities of the high school do depart from the intellectual at times. Everyone is familiar with such common events as the school parties and interscholastic athletics. Certainly, these require no great exercise of the intellect for either the participants or the spectators. They are nonintellectual *additions* to the school program, and hence they may occasionally divert someone from intellectual pursuits. They are not the result of deliberate anti-intellectual intentions.

The nonintellectual activities of the high school are truly modest in comparison with the extravagant spectacles common on college and university campuses. Both mathematics *and* football are developed more fully on the college level than in the high school. Even the most venerable and academic collegiate institutions are likely to receive more space on the sports page than in all of the rest of the newspaper. Yet they escape the charge of anti-intellectualism. Perhaps it is a charge that college teachers would rather hurl at the high schools than at each other.

Surely it is not at all remarkable that high schools and colleges are so much alike in this respect. They have the same students and are influenced by the same cultural patterns and trends. Both institutions make intellectual programs available to their students, both offer many other courses which are less intellectual in nature, and, in both, students enjoy a variety of nonintellectual activities.

INTELLECTUALISM PLUS

A substantial segment of the high-school population, consisting of those who take the college preparatory curricula, study the difficult, abstract courses. Undoubtedly, this is intellectualism. A great many others take courses of lesser intellectual quality. All students, at one time or another, participate in nonintellectual activities. This is not anti-intellectualism. It is more accurate to describe the situation as *intellectualism plus* other elements. The essentially academic character of the high school of pleasant reminiscence has been retained as one phase of the modern American secondary school. Other equally necessary, but less revered, phases have been added to make the high school a comprehensive institution for all American youth. The classical curriculum has not been destroyed, although it has been trimmed somewhat. Most of it remains as one of the several avenues available to students.

Public opinion has demanded and received such new high-school courses as vocational agriculture and homemaking and such curricula as the commercial and vocational. Unfortunately, human vision has not always expanded to match the widening scope of modern secondary education. And so the curricula that come the nearest to meeting the educational needs of those who are not going to college are regarded as assaults upon intellectualism. It would be just as illogical to criticize the teaching of foreign languages as an attack upon vocational education. Failure to see the whole of the high-school curriculum as well as its many parts has been responsible for the current misconception of the American high school.

THE TRUE STORY OF LIFE ADJUSTMENT EDUCATION

The story of life adjustment education is a convenient illustration of the ease with which misconceptions are formed when an entire educational institution is judged by only one of its many phases, and when even that is not understood very well. The term *life adjustment* first appeared in the professional literature of education near the end of World War II as a phrase describing the type of secondary education which seemed to be necessary for the majority of students. Tremendous increases in secondary school enrollments in the first four decades of the twentieth century had made it clear that the traditional curriculum of the formerly selective high school must be adapted for the education of *all* American youth. In 1944 when the phrase "life adjustment" first appeared, about 20 percent of all high-school students entered college; nearly all of them, and thousands of others, were enrolled in the college preparatory curriculum. Approximately 20 percent more were in vocational curricula leading toward the skilled occupations. Neither the college preparatory nor the vocational curricula properly served the educational needs of the remaining 60 percent, and it was *for these students* that life adjustment education was contemplated. It was proposed as a type of general education that would be more useful *for them* than either the traditional academic or the specialized vocational courses.

The beginning of a more functional curriculum for American secondary education had appeared in the first two decades of the twentieth century as a general movement toward curricular reorganization. Life adjustment education was a logical development in the reorganization movement which had continued to expand through the 1920's and 1930's as school people sought to provide useful learning experiences for *all* of the millions of youth who entered the nation's high schools. These were decades in which many additions and modifications were made in the curriculum.

Life adjustment education, as one phase of the high-school program, does not threaten the college preparatory and vocational curricula. Both of these are securely established with multitudes of advocates. It can supplement them, however, by adding comprehensiveness to the total program of the American secondary school. It can provide useful high-school education for the non-academic, nonvocationally minded students who comprise a large portion of the total enrollment. These students entered the high school before it was ready to educate them. Perhaps it was necessary for several generations of them to struggle through courses which were inadequate for them, to the exasperation of many of their teachers, until their need for a different type of secondary education became unmistakably clear.

A primary purpose of life adjustment education is to provide more useful learning experiences for all such students. This means a type of English instruction that is more practical than the diagramming of sentences and the detailed study of literary classics; science and mathematics taught in application to the events of day-by-day living; and civics and history which can be put into immediate practice in the responsibilities and rights of citizenship. This in no way interferes with more abstract study of any of these subjects by other students.

There can be no doubt that the subject matter of such functional courses can be learned more easily than the materials of the traditional academic subjects. This is in accord with their purpose, for most of the students for whom life adjustment education has been proposed can be expected to have little success in learning abstract subject matter and in applying it to the problems which will confront them after they leave the school. They are much better off studying materials which they can learn and which they can also learn to use.

Life adjustment education can aid all students to learn more about themselves and their relationships with others in the vast areas of personal and family problems which are scarcely mentioned in the college preparatory and vocational curricula. These valuable learnings do not detract in any way from the thoroughness of preparation either for college or for a skilled occupation. They are likely to make specific learnings more functional for the situations in which they are to be used. This is a second supplementary aspect of life adjustment education, adding to the usefulness of high-school education for all students, whether they be concentrating on vocational *or* college preparation.

As the years continue to bring changes in American

society, and in the public schools which serve it, revisions may also be expected in life adjustment education. It is probable that the original ratio of 20-60-20 (for the entire nation and hence unlikely to fit many local situations) will be altered as larger numbers of high-school graduates go to college. But the exact ratio is of little importance. What is important is that the value of life adjustment education is likely to undergo steady improvement through analysis and revision by professional educators.

Life adjustment education is commonly misconstrued as the entire high-school curriculum for all students. This view reveals a poor understanding of its true scope and purpose. Yet this is the conception of life adjustment education which has appeared so frequently, and which has been the grounds for its harshest criticisms. The proposal has been attacked as though its purpose were to lure students who should take the college preparatory subjects away from them. It should be obvious, however, that the study of functional curricula by students of limited ability will never prevent brighter students from taking the more difficult subjects whenever they are convinced of their present and future values. Nor will the study of personal and social problems by all youth keep any of them away from the established courses in science and mathematics if they belong there.

The entire curriculum of the secondary school cannot be evaluated by criticisms of only one of its many phases, whether it be life adjustment education, physics, or shorthand and typing. Yet this has been attempted over and over again. The high school in general has been criticized severely because of the purposes and

learning activities of life adjustment education, with little or no mention of the other concurrent phases of the
curriculum.

THE SCHOOL AND ITS SOCIETY

Every aspect of public education is influenced by the
society which surrounds the school. The attitudes,
ideals, and customs of the society as reflected in the
local community affect the school. Children and youth
bring their home and neighborhood learnings with
them into the corridors and classrooms. There they
respond to the school's efforts with the experiences they
have had in the city, in the village, on the farm, at the
summer camp, and a host of other places. Everything
comes into the school, from illiteracy and delinquency
to culture and charm. And every imaginable shade of
intellectuality is represented.

American communities can hardly be said to be *anti*-
intellectual, for they seldom oppose activities which are
primarily concerned with knowing. They are very often
*non*intellectual, both in the nature of the activities in
which their citizens spend their time and in their lack
of respect for intellectual pursuits. The fictitious ex-
ploits of cowboys and private eyes are read more widely
than Shakespeare and Emerson. Probably both of the
former are watched more frequently on television than
they are read. Few adults continue to find pleasure in
the history and geography to which they were introduced in school. Fewer still keep up in mathematics
and science, unless these have become vocational interests. The foreign languages which were once studied
become little more than memories. Only token respect
is given the intellectual activities of the school.

Much of the present concern for intellectual learning has come in a rather abrupt reversal of what formerly was a very widespread attitude of derision for academic attainments. It must not be forgotten that scorn for the intellectual was quite common in the early years of the 1950's. This was the time in which the term "egghead" was heard everywhere as a mild, but uncomplimentary, epithet for the men who dealt in abstract theory. It was also a time, however, in which professional school people everywhere were improving the intellectual qualities of their institutions. Their ironic reward is to have to witness greater appreciation for the young eggheads they tutored so well than for their own efforts.

The public school is as intellectual as its society permits. In spite of the relatively low regard in which it is held, it is the rational center of most American communities. Always, it tends to operate on a higher intellectual plane than is common in the society about it. This is perhaps the greatest virtue of the school; and it is the source of education's power to improve a civilization by enabling each generation to rise above those which came before.

The legend of anti-intellectualism is the result of an exceedingly narrow view of the modern public school. Criticism has been concentrated upon a few phases of education as though they were the entire instructional program. This has created a mythical image of schools in which few children study anything of a serious nature. The true range of intellectualism which enables the modern school to match its students' diverse capabilities has been ignored. In the haste to blame, too little time has been spent in studying the progress the public schools have made in solving the problems of educating *everyone's* children. A prominent example of the

numerous misapprehensions from which the schools
have suffered is the popular and erroneous conception
of the role of progressive education. A brief review of
the basic principles of progressive education and the
extent of their acceptance in the public schools is presented in the next chapter.

12. The Grand Illusion of Progressive Education

The grandest misconception of all in the spirited debate over the public schools is the complaint that "Progressive Education" has been responsible for deterioration in the quality of learning. Here is folklore, compounded from a collection of misunderstandings, which has become an obsession with many critics. Undoubtedly, it is among the most frequent of criticisms of the public schools. It is also one of the hardiest, for it survives independently of the real teaching that goes on in real schools. Perhaps the secret of its indestructibility is this very separation from fact, for the essence of any folklore is the unreflective quality of the thinking by which it is preserved. The illusion of the pernicious effect of progressive education would dissolve immediately were it exposed to the reality of everyday practices, but the two are so completely separated that the opportunities for illusion to be confronted with fact are very few.

A WHIPPING BOY FOR CRITICS

The prince had his personal whipping boy who took the punishment for the royal heir's misbehavior. Progressivism has been cast in a similar role in many American communities where it has been blamed for circumstances, the true causes for which are inconvenient and embarrassing to identify. Progressive education has become a popular whipping boy in numerous situations where the real faults were insufficient financial support for the schools and too little moral support for the faculty. Let a community ignore its youth problems for a few years until its delinquency figures have risen alarmingly—someone is sure to blame progressive education. Or perhaps the public has refused to approve bond issues for badly needed school buildings. The decline in quality which results from overcrowding can then quickly be attributed to progressive education. Who has not heard or read statements to the effect that all that is really needed in public education today is a return to old-fashioned methods and elimination of the "frills" of the curriculum?

Such evasions of reality are often rich in metaphor. The school subjects have been "softened up" or "watered down" because of the influence of progressive education. Subject matter which has been "predigested," is "spoon fed" to youngsters in "catering" to their interests. The curriculum has "suffered"; it has been "eroded away" by "modern theories" of education. The obvious remedy is to "beef up" the curriculum by giving students something "they can sink their teeth into," thus exercising their "flabby minds" and "sharpening their mental powers."

None of the items in this metaphorical mishmash is at all descriptive or explanatory in nature. They add nothing to understanding the processes of teaching and learning that take place in the public schools. Nor do they explain the purposes of progressive education; they ignore some very unsatisfactory conditions in the traditional curriculum that led to the movement of progressive education. But they are convenient labels of derogation for anyone who is not well enough acquainted with the schools to describe them accurately. To use a metaphor, they are the lashes with which the whipping boy is flayed.

So much undeserved blame has been cast at progressive education that the term has lost its usefulness. It can hardly be mentioned in any current discussion of schools without arousing so much emotion that any objective consideration of the issues is almost impossible. For many persons today, progressive education is nothing more than a derogatory expression for any unapproved procedure. Use of the term almost certainly identifies the speaker's opposition to modern education. Condemnation of the progressive movement has even descended to the level of characterizing it as un-American.

Progressive education, like many other innovations, began as a reaction against traditional practices. Dissatisfaction with established systems has been responsible for many proposals for change in the field of education, as elsewhere. If the proposals are consistent and attract a sizeable following, they can in time exert a considerable influence upon the practices they oppose. Very often the eventual result is modification of the older practices to include some of the newer proposals, instead of a complete change in procedures. This has happened with the ideas of progressive education, with a great deal of local variation in the extent to which modifications have been made.

THE COMMON SENSE PURPOSES OF PROGRESSIVE EDUCATION

The progressive education movement originated as an attempt to reform the traditional curriculum by the introduction of changes based upon studies of the school in its society. The movement began shortly before 1920. At that time, three factors of great importance to public education had already been identified. One was the rapid rate of change in American culture, symbolized by the appearance of the airplane and automobile. Another was increased knowledge of the processes of learning. The third factor was the changing composition of the secondary school population.

Consideration of these factors led to grave doubts of the suitability of traditional teaching methods and content for the educational needs of American children and youth. From such doubts came the impetus to change. The direction of that change has been guided throughout by scientific studies of learning, teaching, and cultural changes. The movement has been a thoroughgoing search for progress in American education.

But progress in general terms requires specific changes in procedures. Any description of the changes which have been sought must be somewhat arbitrary, since educators, like other persons, do not always agree upon their ideas of progress. The list below presents five fundamental changes which have been urged in the name of progress in education on which most professionals would agree. Each proposed change is presented in contrast to the traditional educational practices against which it has been a reaction:

1. To provide learning experiences which appeal to the natural interests of children, and lead to the development of additional desirable interests, *instead* of presenting a fixed, unvarying content.
2. To permit children to share in planning their own learning experiences *instead* of limiting them entirely to adult-chosen activities.
3. To vary instruction for individual children and groups of children to serve their studied and understood needs, *instead* of teaching the same content at the same pace to all of them.
4. To teach with the aim of promoting a better understanding of the relationships among subjects and to the home and community, *instead* of separating the subjects completely from each other and from life outside the school.
5. To teach through a variety of learning experiences, *instead* of through the single experience of studying a textbook.

These are exactly the kind of common-sense proposals that most parents approve in their conversations with teachers and in community conferences on education. The majority of parents are pleased when their children participate in learning activities such as those just listed. They are likely to be more pleased if the activities are merely described, however, than if they are referred to as progressive. Remarks such as, "Why didn't they do that when I was in school?" and "I wish I could have had that," are often heard as adults learn of the work their children have done in schools where these procedures are followed.

Surely the most unjust criticism of all is that progressive education is un-American, for the origins of the movement were wholly within this country. Educational

innovations such as those described above are wholesome expressions of the finest American ideals. They
convey to students the promise of more opportunities
for the exercise of personal initiative, independent judgment, and creative thinking. These are the qualities that
made the United States a great democratic nation. They
are also the qualities necessary for it to continue to
grow in greatness and in democracy. The application of
the term un-American to such practices exemplifies that
kind of upside down thinking from which folklore is
produced.

Even the above brief descriptions of progressive education's innovations will help fill the void of understanding which remains when the supply of derogatory
metaphors has been exhausted. However, a little more
information on each of the five purposes will add details for further understanding.

THE PROPER UNDERSTANDING OF INTEREST

The interests of children were seldom considered as
assets in the schools of the proverbial Golden Age.
More likely, they were thought of as disturbing influences against which the teacher must be on guard at
all times. The content of subjects was formal and inflexible, and it was the same for every child in every
class. Subject matter had little meaning for a great
many youngsters, who found nothing in it they could
enjoy. This, however, was often regarded as an advantage; the belief that it was good for children to do
things they did not like to do was widely held. The
lessons of the classroom corresponded to little that was
naturally interesting to the children themselves. Small
wonder that children were reluctant to enter school. Is

it not also more than coincidence that physical punishment was very common in the classroom?

Many educators rebelled against this sort of teaching. They saw real disadvantages in forcing children to study lessons which had no appeal. They observed the remarkable lengths to which children went to expend their time and effort in the satisfaction of their interests. Then, as now, the classroom shirker often displayed great energy away from school. So the logical question came to be asked: "Would it not be possible to channel into the classroom the tremendous amounts of effort which children willingly give to the activities in which they engage because of their own interests?" Imaginative minds began to consider the interests of children as they planned lessons. How could the study of history, geography, grammar, and other subjects be motivated by relating them to things which were exciting to children?

This does not mean that interest was ever intended to *be* the curriculum. The often-quoted remark of the disillusioned child, "Do we have to do what we want to do today?" is a fictitious illustration of an extreme situation which no actual classroom has ever approached. It is not "catering" to interests to permit children to select, as part of their reading, books they will enjoy, and to allow them to write compositions on the topics they talk about with friends and parents. Interest permeating the curriculum generates incentive. Use of the dictionary has little appeal in itself, but it can become absorbing when it is considered essential to satisfy another interest. This is curriculum improvement in action.

Good teaching never stops with the interests children bring with them into the school. It also seeks to develop new and more advanced interests from the learning activities of the classroom. In good teaching the lessons are planned not only to cover subject matter, but also to help children create interests of better quality than those they have developed alone. This is often done in English classes, for example, when teachers make assignments which are intended to improve reading choices by leading children from the literature they already know and like to other writings of greater worth. In subjects such as algebra, in which the content is different from anything students have experienced before, they must be helped to create entirely new interests.

Interests which have been developed in the school have the same potential motivation as any others. All interests have been learned in experiences somewhere. It makes little difference, as far as incentive to learning is concerned, whether the developing experiences occurred in or outside the school. The intensity of the interest, not its source, determines its strength as motivation. The real differences are in quality. Interests which children have developed outside the school are often of questionable value, while those which they have created with the teacher's guidance can be approved by everyone.

PARTNERS IN PLANNING

Permitting children and youth to share in planning their own learning activities is a reliable technique for releasing their energies. One of the most universal of human traits is willingness of people to work more wholeheartedly at tasks they have set for themselves than at duties someone else has assigned to them.

Everyone has noticed that the student who stays with a book of his own choice to the end is often tempted to lay aside his homework before it has been completed. Similarly, adults frequently work harder at their hobbies than at their jobs. Nearly all of us will place the highest priorities on the tasks of our own choosing.

Many situations in teaching afford opportunities for students to share in planning classroom activities. Even within the limits set by a State Department syllabus and a local course of study, innumerable choices can be made in the teaching of any grade or subject. Among these are the number of days to be spent on a chapter, the division of the class period into such activities as discussion and supervised study, the titles of books for outside reading, the subjects for compositions and book reports, and even the lengths of assignments. In the traditional school, these and all other decisions were made by the teachers. Most students were not even aware that choices were being made. They accepted the teacher's pronouncements with much the same complaining, but unquestioning, attitudes as they witnessed the regular passage of the days and weeks of the school term. Decision-making today can be a cooperative process involving teachers and students, but the extent of student participation varies greatly among local school systems and among the teachers within a system. Student influence upon decisions is almost always quite limited, which is proper in view of their lack of experience and maturity, but even minor choices can bring to a school subject the motivation that comes from setting one's own goals.

A common situation in nearly any class in mathematics will illustrate how easily students can share in making a decision. In this case, the first part of the class period has been used to check the assignment made the day before, and the most difficult problems have been put on the blackboard by students who have solved them. A few more minutes have been spent in the demonstration of the type of problems which will be assigned for the next day. Fifteen minutes remain in the period. How shall the time be used? This is the kind of decision teachers make every day, often without realizing that a choice has been made. Several alternatives are both possible and useful. The time can be used for review of material previously covered, for drill on current problems, for study of the next day's assignment, or to present more new material. It is quite reasonable for the teacher to make the decision alone, but it is equally appropriate to permit the class to share in the choice by asking them for suggestions for the use of the remaining time.

Their individual responses will be on about the same level as the rest of their work in the class. Most students will have serious suggestions, but the class wits are likely to maintain their roles by proposing sleep or a soda break. Some time may be spent in debate if this is the first occasion on which their advice has been asked, but as the situation is repeated they will learn to make group choices quickly and responsibly. The feeling of sharing in the decision will also enhance class morale. One of the recurring surprises in this kind of teaching is observing students propose longer assignments than the teacher had planned for them.

Valuable learnings in self-direction result from students' experiences in sharing classroom decisions. People learn to make decisions by making them. Unless some opportunities for making decisions are given young people while they are at school, it is hardly logical to

expect responsible choices from them immediately after-
ward. Both common sense and progress in education
would therefore seem to demand a gradual increase in
the number and importance of the decisions students
are permitted to make as they mature from children to
adults.

Participation in planning sometimes occurs in other
less desirable ways. Youngsters have always engaged in a
certain amount of unsanctioned planning. Most adults
can recall at least one time when the class succeeded
in postponing an assigned test by asking the teacher
questions until the period was nearly over. Or perhaps
they remember the day one of the boys adjusted the
thermostat while the teacher was out of the room, thus
making the temperature too high or too low for comfort. Probably most of us enjoy these memories more
than we do the thoughts of our own sons and daughters
occupied in similar planning now.

TEACHING FOR KNOWN NEEDS

Enormous amounts of time and energy have been
spent studying the educational needs of children and
youth. Men of every era have made proposals for the
proper education of the young under such varying designations as principles, needs, and tasks. A great many
listings of such items are contained in the professional
literature of education, all of them together comprising
a catalog of gradual processes of enlargement and re-
finement which will undoubtedly continue to be advocated in the growing literature of the future.

Anyone familiar with the public schools is bound to
notice some discrepancies between the curriculum and
the scholars' proposals. Both the content and the lan-

234 AMERICAN EDUCATION

guage patterns are different. For one thing, schools teach in terms of subjects, and subjects are rarely mentioned in lists of educational needs. For another, economic self-sufficiency or its equivalent is a popular objective of education, but it is hard to find it on the daily schedule of the school. Compilations of needs are general in nature; the materials that are taught in the schools are real and specific. The discrepancies are not total, however. There are, in fact, some conspicuous similarities.

Lists of educational needs and the curriculum coincide most noticeably in the two areas of the fundamental learnings and preparation for college. Both are prominent in the efforts of every public school, and both have appeared in most general presentations of educational needs. These two objectives have dominated the public-school curriculum for many years. Schools come closer to satisfying them for the majority of students than they do in other aspects of their work.

Other kinds of educational needs are seldom served as well as those which are met by teaching the fundamental processes and the subjects required for admission to college, although they are just as valid and a great deal is known about them. Above all, there are the often neglected needs of training in sound personal and social habits and good citizenship. Many persons can develop satisfactory personal and social attributes without the aid of the school, but a very large number of pupils need responsible guidance in these areas. Individual differences probably are even greater here than in the learning of arithmetic and spelling, for many children come to the school from very difficult home and neighborhood conditions.

The development of healthy personal and social attitudes is often referred to as personality adjustment. Although the need for it is evidenced by the presence in most schools of more maladjusted children than can be handled, something about the term seems to irritate many persons. The whole concept of adjustment has become a focal point for criticisms of the schools. Teachers are even accused of teaching "adjustment" instead of subjects. The volume and intensity of the attacks would indicate widespread belief either that youngsters can solve all of their personal and social problems alone, or that an individual's personal traits have no effect on his learning. Of course, both of these propositions collapse when they are exposed to the known facts of mental illness in present-day American life. Adults as well as children so frequently need guidance that the demand for these professional services has been growing rapidly. The effects of personal difficulties upon work and learning have become so well known that they are now recognized as serious problems in every sphere of American life.

Genuine progress is made in education when instruction is planned to serve the known needs of the children in the classroom. Subject matter which is identical for everyone in a given class will be inadequate for some pupils and too difficult for others. The English teaching which is most suitable for a seventh-grade class in one section of a city may be wholly inappropriate for a group of seventh graders in another part of the same community. The older schools attempted to teach uniformly for all students. The use of modern techniques can enable the faculties of today's schools to understand children's real needs and adapt instruction to serve them.

LEARNING THAT MEANS SOMETHING

All of the subjects taught in the schools are artificial divisions of knowledge, made for convenience and efficiency. Unquestionably, it is more convenient to teach them separately, and usually it is more efficient. However, efficiency sometimes reaches the point where ability to use the tools of a subject gets ahead of the child's understanding of it. Students often develop skill in processes without learning the uses for which they are intended. Few problems outside the school come neatly labeled as English or mathematics or history. In most situations, classification of a problem helps to determine the type of knowledge needed to solve it; often the classification is more difficult than the solution. One must know when, as well as how, to multiply, if arithmetic is to be very useful.

English and history are separate subjects in about 95 percent of American high schools, but they are never separated for the citizen who needs the skills and understandings of his native language to interpret the history that is made during his lifetime. Similarly, the scientist who has studied chemistry and English and mathematics separately needs to use them together in his profession.

Little thought was given to the relationships among subjects in the traditional school. Students were "on their own" when it came to applying their learning. Even less attention was paid to the use of school learnings in home and community situations. High-school graduates, even those who had excelled in science and history, were often ignorant of the operations of the appliances in their homes and the governments in their communities. Even today, it is unusual to find college freshmen who have any real understanding of either the American family or the American community. Yet these are the most important social institutions in their lives.

The personal and social values of education can be enhanced immeasurably by teaching students an understanding of the relevancy of their learning in the different subdivisions of knowledge. No one in any vocation works exclusively with the specialized skills and knowledges of his calling, and people from all occupations meet on the common ground of citizenship. Almost everyone has a family as well as a career, and who would say that the former is the less important of the two?

LEARNING FROM MANY SOURCES

Modern education has made tremendous gains in the number and variety of the teaching aids which are used to enrich instruction. The textbook has retained its popularity as a source of learning, but it has been supplemented extensively everywhere. Such devices as films, filmstrips, tape recorders, record players, maps, globes, charts, and models are prominent features of the modern classroom. But their use has not been at the expense of reading, in which supplementary assignments have also been increased in number and improved in quality. Microfilmed books and newspapers are available to many high-school students, and they are more conveniently used than the original copies. Students in today's schools learn from a much wider variety of materials than did their parents and grandparents. The result is better education in at least two respects.

Learning is more efficient when subject matter can be

presented in several forms than when only one is possible. For example, hearing and seeing reinforce reading to increase learning. Studying a globe adds to the meaning of a textbook, and viewing a film adds even more. Hearing excellent recorded speech increases the learnings which can be obtained from the student's own reading and speaking efforts. Educators use the term *multisensory* to describe learnings which are received through several different kinds of perception.

Use of the numerous teaching aids which were mentioned above enables teachers to present subject matter in the ways which are most efficient for learning, and to present it in more than one form. The use of teaching aids also helps to avoid the excesses of verbalism in which words are memorized with little knowledge of their meaning.

A second advantage of the use of many kinds of teaching aids is the opportunity they afford students to make comparisons of materials. It has always been difficult to prevent uncritical acceptance of the viewpoints of the textbook when it was the only source of information. "It's so because the book says so" has been a very common attitude among students in the past. It appears less frequently today because the practice of using many sources of information has become more feasible.

More actual progress has been made in expanding the variety of learning aids than in any other basic purpose of progressive education. Nearly all colleges in which teachers are educated now offer courses in the use of audio-visual aids to learning, and an impressive amount of professional literature has been produced on the subject. Extensive use of teaching aids has become routine in even the most conservative schools. There can be no doubt that school people are thoroughly convinced of their efficiency in increasing the quality and quantity of learning. A city school system today is expected to maintain a central film library and to employ one or more audio-visual specialists. Individual schools usually have their own libraries of filmstrips, often to the number of five or six hundred. Albums of records to be played in English, typing, foreign languages, and social studies classes usually remain in the classrooms where they are needed.

DISCREDITING THROUGH DISTORTION

It seems incredible, as one examines the common-sense proposals of progressive education, that the movement could ever have lost its good repute. Yet, in spite of its sound and obvious merits, the most common usage of the term "progressive education" today is uncomplimentary. It is so generally heard in this sense that educators have learned to substitute unemotional phrases descriptive of school activities. A public which shrinks from "progressive education" will often ask for the employment of additional school personnel to study the needs of children and counsel them in their personal and social problems when such services are called guidance. Many of the same parents who admire certain teachers because they have been able to interest their children in school and work would not knowingly approve the hiring of a "progressive" teacher. Twenty years ago, the word "progressive" was a compliment in educational cricles; at the present time, it is more apt to be a condemnation.

All of this has happened because the sound principles of progressive education have been grossly distorted into fantastic exaggerations of the originals. The basic devotion to children's interests, shared planning, study of needs, reality of experiences, and variety of learning materials has been converted into a monstrous caricature: a nation's schools at the mercy of infantile whimsies. The inherent falsity of the caricature has not prevented it from capturing public opinion. Very likely this wholesale seizure of the general imagination has been easier because of Americans' tendency to caricature their schoolmasters. Our national literature contains many unkind parodies of the teacher, and he has often been exposed to ridicule under the guise of humor. The result of the caricature has been serious damage to the effectiveness of progressive principles, and some fantastic additions to the folklore of education.

THE SPARSE SYMBOLS OF EXCELLENCE

The fact is that the principles of progressive education have won only very limited acceptance in the public schools. The overwhelming majority of the schools remain conservative in most respects. In pronounced contrast to the progressive proposals described earlier in this chapter, the classroom experiences of most American children are planned for them in advance by adults. Usually all the children in a class study the same assignments from the same textbooks at the same time. Typically, each subject is separate and distinct from all others. The single exception now in large-scale use is the supplementation of reading with mechanical teaching aids. The textbook, however, continues to dominate the American classroom. It is still the major source of classroom learning for the great majority of American children. The allegation that the public schools have turned progressive is pure myth. The probability is at least 100 to 1 that anyone who complains about the quality of education in his local community is criticizing a school which is essentially conservative.

Yet the methods of progressive education are the hallmarks of excellence in the rather small number of schools where they are in use. Their results, as has been demonstrated repeatedly, are better education for children and youth. Nor is progressive education an attribute of the "easy" school. The latter type of institution will almost invariably be found to be extremely conservative and to suffer from inadequate resources in such respects as financial support and continuity of teaching by well-qualified personnel. Nothing in the theory of progressive education condones laxity. In fact, its students usually do more and better work than is done in other schools where the ideas of progressive education have not gained acceptance. Least of all can progressivism be associated with any form of hoodlumism. Juvenile delinquency is not a product of progressive education.

At the present time, progressive education has been tried on a very limited scale in the public schools, and where it has been tried its results have been found highly satisfactory. Its practices will probably continue to spread, even as the term itself fades from use. It is also very likely that any antagonism to truly progressive education will diminish with the disappearance of the term. Both the public and the teaching profession will desire more of the good results which a small percentage of schools now enjoy. The diffusion of practices may be expected to move rather slowly, as has been the case with nearly all innovations in American education, although the pace has accelerated in recent years. Perhaps in another decade or two, the sound methods of progressive education will be exhibited with pride as a "return to fundamentals."

Denunciation of progressive education rarely exhausts the critic's dissatisfaction with the public schools. More often than not, a description of the supposed faults of the progressive movement shifts into a brisk attack upon the professional courses in teacher education which are presumed to be its source. The more common criticisms of these courses reveal some interesting patterns of reaching conclusions about the teaching in the colleges' departments of education. A notable amount of folklore is also displayed. An examination of the criticisms of teacher education and of its real problems forms the content of Chapter XIII.

13. Those Maligned Education Courses

Some of the most savage attacks in the history of American education have been directed at the professional courses college students must take for teacher certification. It is charged that they are so simple-minded that students inevitably view them as the "snap" courses on the campus and that, besides, they go over the same subject matter again and again. Both criticisms imply that there is some degree of merit to the courses, while protesting the amount of time consumed. Presumably both could be satisfied by combining and reducing the number of courses in education. Other critics would go much further: abolish the professional courses entirely as being wholly impractical and unnecessary, on the theory that anyone who knows a subject well can teach it well.

The several forms of criticism of teacher education are more impressive in volume than in accuracy; nearly all are examples of an unreflective "folklore" attitude toward education. It is useful to examine them because of the wide attention they have received and because of the lack of understanding they reveal. But first let us consider the status, origin, and nature of the courses in question.

THE PROFESSIONAL COURSES IN EDUCATION

The subject matter of education courses is education, not science or history or literature. Such courses are taught in the departments of education by professors of education, and are seldom taken by students who are preparing for careers other than teaching. They add the "how" and "when" of teaching to the "what" already learned in other college courses. Education courses are firmly established (too firmly to please some critics) in the curricula of colleges training public school teachers. All states now require approximately twenty semester-hours of credit in education for teaching certification. Though since the war thousands of emergency certificates have been issued to alleviate the severe teacher shortage, these have been but temporary exceptions to the regular licensing procedures. The required education of career teachers still includes the full array of professional courses.

Most instruction in the art or science of teaching is of fairly recent origin. Forty years ago one could teach in the public schools of many states with little or no such preparation. The embryonic profession of education had made only modest beginnings in what have since become full-blown professional courses. As more was learned about educating chldren, new courses were developed and added to the certification requirements of the states. Specialized, advanced courses were created for those wishing to prepare for careers in guidance and administration, and some of the states began to require specific certification for these positions. A distinct sequence of professional courses leading to state certification is now offered for every type of position in public school teaching and administration.

Some critics who have proclaimed the superiority of schools of half a century ago over those of today have based their arguments in part on the absence of professional teacher training in those days, while conveniently forgetting—or ignoring—that the academic education of these teachers was often equally limited. Academic prerequisites for teaching have increased along with professional ones. Forty years ago graduates of an eight-year elementary school could still enter the normal school—the precursor of the teachers college—study there for as little as two years, and return as teachers to the elementary school. Admirable though they were in many respects, it is brash indeed to claim that those teen-agers were better teachers than today's professionals with their four or five years of college education—as brash a contention with regard to teaching as it would be for any other modern profession. Nor were some of the high-school teachers of forty years ago much better off: many had had scarcely more education than their students. It was not unusual to go into teaching after only a year or two of college, and once in a while someone who had never graduated from the twelfth grade moved up the teaching ladder from the elementary grades into high school. Insufficient education was most common, of course, among teachers who had begun their careers in the first few years of the century or even earlier.

THE SECONDARY TEACHER'S EDUCATION

Modern teacher education makes a clear distinction, in professional training, between elementary and secondary teachers. Professional courses in secondary education account for approximately one-sixth of the four years of undergraduate work required for the bachelor's degree. This totals about twenty semester-hours of credit in institutions dividing the academic year into two semesters, or about thirty term-hours of credit in those dividing the year into three terms. Variations of about 20 percent from the average among the different states create a range of sixteen to twenty-four semester-hours of professional courses. Fewer variations occur within any one state, where all graduates must meet the same set of certification requirements.

A typical sequence of education courses for the prospective secondary school teacher divides his twenty semester-hours of study among courses in orientation to teaching, educational psychology, tests and measurements, guidance, general methods of teaching, special methods of teaching in his major field, and student teaching. All except the student teaching, which usually covers five or six semester-hours of credit, would be two- or three-hour courses. This is a planned sequence covering the essential phases of teaching, in which study of the theory of education culminates in actual teaching practice under the supervision of a capable professional.

But this is only the preparation for a teaching career. A fifth year of study, usually leading to the master's degree, has become almost standard for high-school teaching. Salary schedules everywhere offer higher rates of pay for the master's degree, and thus encourage its attainment. A few states even require the fifth year of study for permanent certification for teaching. Some classroom teachers—and their number is increasing—have gone on to earn the doctor's degree, for which some salary schedules further reward them.

EDUCATION FOR ELEMENTARY TEACHING

Although prospective elementary teachers usually take a similar sequence of education courses, the time devoted to such courses often amounts to as much as one-third of the four-year college curriculum. The added courses reflect the differences in the organizations of the elementary and secondary schools. The high-school teacher is a specialist in one or two subject fields; the elementary teacher must teach many subjects.

In most secondary schools, only English teachers will have taken courses in the special methods of teaching English, and only mathematics teachers will have studied special methods in mathematics, and so on. Each teacher will have taken one or more methods courses in his own field of specialization. But an elementary school teacher, who is assigned to an entire school grade, requires special methods courses in each of the subjects to be taught. Separate courses in special methods in English, reading, arithmetic, social studies, science, art, and music add many semester-hours to the curriculum. The number may be reduced slightly by combining English and reading or social studies and science in a single course, but each of these really deserves independent status.

All special methods courses, whether for elementary or secondary teachers, include a considerable amount of academic subject matter. No one can study the methods of teaching history, for example, without learning more history in the process. Just as every teacher learns more about his subject as he organizes and presents it, so does every future teacher increase his knowledge of a subject as he studies the methods of teaching it.

CAN THE DISTINGUISHED PROFESSOR TEACH ARITHMETIC?

One of the favorite ploys used in attacking the professional courses in education is to mention the name of the most distinguished mathematician who comes to mind and lament the fact that certification requirements would not permit him to teach arithmetic in the elementary school. This is apparently intended as a crushing demonstration of the fallacy of requiring people to learn how to teach before licensing them. It is exceedingly probable, however, that this "Looky-Looky" statement, "Professor Eminence cannot teach arithmetic in the public schools," is true in more ways than contemplated. Teaching arithmetic effectively to thirty children requires specific skills that the professor is not likely to have had opportunities to develop. One suspects that he would prefer not to make the attempt.

State certification requirements represent the best efforts to date to protect youngsters from unqualified teachers. They are as appropriate in education as licensing procedures are in any other profession. They do not threaten the academic disciplines. Any detailed study of them will reveal that they maintain a balance between academic and education courses and thus prevent inadequacies in content or method. Certification requirements are not the results of a conspiracy among educators; they have been established openly and legitimately, and they have been revised whenever necessary. They are the school's strongest bulwark.

THE DEEP, WIDE CHASM

The most bitter feelings against courses in education lodge in the breasts of members of other academic departments. Not only do the criticisms from this source make most others seem mild by comparison, but they are the most deeply resented by professors of education. The resulting difference of opinion often becomes so strong that effective communication is almost impossible. Though the width and depth of the gulf vary from one institution to another, a permanent division between departments of education and the other academic departments is characteristic of American colleges. It is also present in the teachers colleges, which are often mistakenly held to be staffed wholly by professional educators. Clashes are intensified in curriculum committees and faculty meetings, where the request for a new course in education may bring the opposition of other departments into the open, while professors of education seek to rally their friends in support. The disputes have even been known to enter classrooms as argumentative lectures by faculty protagonists before their captive audiences. Each controversy widens and deepens the chasm until eventually objective consideration of the merits of a new course succumbs to partisanship.

The critics of education courses have a tactical advantage in the conflict: most of the battles are not fought on their home grounds. Educators are less likely to be called on to attack a new course in mathematics than to defend an innovation in their own department. Inevitably the conflicts reach the pages of the professional magazines, and even books, where they make lively reading. Several college professors of other disciplines, such as history and English, have written books in criticism of public education, but no professor of education has yet written a book denouncing the teaching of history or English.

The unhappy chasm appears not only to be permanent, but to be growing wider and deeper. One of the unfortunate consequences has been the tendency for scholars distinguished in their own fields to be less scholarly in their efforts to discredit the work of fields other than their own, and thereby to contribute to the prevalent "folklore" of education. The problems of public education are complex and difficult. No one, no matter how able in his own field, who has not read and observed widely and with discrimination in education, has qualified himself as an authority. Far too often a contemporary critic starts with a specific, "Once I observed a class that . . ." statement and springboards to a general condemnation of modern education. From such thinking is folklore created.

Both sides of the intramural division between education and the academic departments include individuals of good will who abstain from such acrimonious disputes as they seek to strengthen the entire programs of their institutions. They probably outnumber the actual disputants, and their presence on the campuses is evidence that mutual understanding and cooperation in the problems concerning professional education and liberal arts are attainable. More such men and women are needed, for the best contributions of the academicians and educators alike are essential to good teacher education.

PLEASING THE PROFESSOR

A byproduct of the process of education is the art of telling the instructor what he wants to hear. Proficiency in this art increases as students progress through school. Little fellows in the primary grades are often blunt in expressing disapproval of the teacher, but they soon learn better, and most of them are quite adept at saying the right thing by the time they reach college. Most artful of all are the graduate students. They have developed not only the understandable ability to flatter the professor in speaking well of his courses and writings, but that of knocking his competitors for him as well. It is plain that they firmly believe this enhances their opportunities for favorable consideration in such important matters as grades, fellowships, job openings, and promotions. Most professors, aware of the technique of "apple polishing," identify and discount much of it.

Apparently, certain graduate students have recently confided a great deal to certain academic professors about education courses. (Like all good salesmen, they seem to have chosen their prospects carefully.) The students have been reported as saying that the education courses are so easy that they avoid them—a truly remarkable attitude in at least two respects. First, it is about as complete a reversal of student behavior as one could possibly imagine. For generations college students have discovered the "snap" courses on the campus and passed this useful information along to others. Are they now advising one another to take only the hardest courses? Secondly, these very students are the graduates of the same public high schools the critical professors have condemned as anti-intellectual. Obviously their early years in college effected miracles in developing such an aversion to easy courses.

But professors of education also are susceptible to the blandishment of their students. They too have occasion to listen to remarks about the courses on the other side of the chasm, and the slightest indication of relish for these comments will immediately multiply their volume. As can easily be surmised, such statements consistently cater to what is known of the listener's own beliefs; they are intended to tell him what he wants to hear. So far no professional educators have published anything purportedly learned from students about other professors' courses. It is to be hoped that their admirable silence in this respect will not be broken; hearsay evidence is always suspect, and this particular form of hearsay is especially vulnerable.

THE PROFESSIONAL EDUCATOR'S UNIQUE POSITION

The training of the professor of education qualifies him to make some interesting comparisons between the courses of his department and those of the other departments on the campus. His position is unique: he has taken more courses on the other side of the divide than on his own. From two-thirds to five-sixths of his four-year undergraduate work, and very likely some of his graduate work, was done in departments other than education. Thus he can compare at first hand the courses in other fields with those he has taken and taught in the field of education. He alone on the campus possesses such a comprehensive background. No academic professor has had experience in education equal to the educator's experience in the other departments. The educator has taken many of their courses, but few of them have taken any of his.

The professor of education holds another important advantage: by education *and* experience, by theory *and* practice, he is a specialist in education; others specialize only in the subject matter of their departments. Teaching is not only his profession, but his subject matter as well. He is the actual practitioner of the art he teaches. A similar situation could occur in another department, as when a professor of mathematics gives courses in the teaching of mathematics, but though this happens occasionally in the state teachers colleges, it is infrequent in the universities.

NO MONOPOLY ON MERIT

The educator understands the strengths and weaknesses of the courses in education better than anyone else possibly can. He is qualified to judge teaching, and the results of his teaching are all about him every day. He knows also that no department has a monopoly on merit. On most campuses all students use the same library, and the professor has ample opportunity of observing their use of reference materials. He notices that his students usually do about as well in their other classes as in education.

The facts are that good and poor courses are to be found everywhere. They defy attempts at classification according to department. Some courses are deadly, even in the most venerable disciplines; others are stimulating, in education as well as elsewhere. No department has a monopoly on "snap" courses. The subject matter of one class is sometimes retaught in another; some college courses even repeat part of the instruction of the high school. But neither ease nor repetition is confined to education departments. Adverse criticism of a single course in education may be valid, and if so, can be verified. Wholesale censure of all education courses is irresponsible.

The accusations directed at the professional courses in education reflect upon college administrators as much as upon the departments of education, for the administration bears the final responsibility for every department on the campus. It is inconceivable that any department would long be permitted to operate on lower levels of quality than the others. Surely any defects peculiar to education would have been corrected as soon as they became evident. It is worthy of note that only rarely have college presidents, who have a broader view, indulged in denunciations of the offerings of whole departments.

THE REAL WEAKNESSES

The real weaknesses of professional education courses are quite unlike those alleged by the critics. The courses are neither too easy nor do they duplicate subject content excessively; in both respects they share the general characteristics of their institutions. One of the two most serious defects in teacher education is the dearth of actual classroom experience during the early courses. Too many teacher education curricula postpone all contact with children until the student teaching of the senior year, when the responsibility is shared with an experienced critic-teacher. Too often the previous professional courses tell by book and lecture *about* children but are devoid of experiences *with* children. Although many strong voices have been raised in favor of more and earlier experiences with children during the college years, relatively little progress has been made in revising the teacher education curricula. The theory of teaching presented in the early professional courses is sound, but it lacks the reality derived from student teaching experiences with children in actual school situations.

Both the theory and the practice of teaching are essential to the preparation of a teacher. Today most teacher education is heavily overbalanced by theory, to the relative neglect of practical experience. A great deal has been said and written on the problem by professional educators (though it has scarcely been mentioned by the critics of public education).

TEACHING BY EXAMPLE

The second of the really serious weaknesses in contemporary teacher education is the failure of the professors of education to use in their own courses the methods they urge on future teachers. Far too many education courses consist solely of lecturing and reading the textbook, and students try to learn to teach by hearing and reading about the problems of teaching. They sit silently through lectures on the need to stimulate their pupils to take part in class discussions, for example. A general class discussion between the professor and the future teachers would be a far more effective and memorable illustration of the methods the student could later use in his own classes. Similarly, a lecture on how junior-high-school pupils can construct relief maps is less useful than a demonstration followed by the actual construction of a relief map by the college student. Ideally, the professor of education would announce to his students that *his* teaching of a given topic is an example of the kind of teaching he recommends for *them*. His use of a film would be a model for their subsequent use of films in the public schools, and his methods of making assignments would be demonstrations of the various methods they could later use. Likewise, each of his tests and examinations would be planned to illustrate sound testing methods as well as to evaluate the learning of his students. If all education courses could be taught in this way, the students' observations of their instructors would enhance immeasurably the listening about teaching that is the chief activity in so much of teacher education today.

One of the clues most used by the young teacher is his memory of the practices of his own teachers—"My history teacher gave us questions to answer as we studied the chapter"; "Miss Model had us write out our oral reports before we gave them in class." This very common imitative tendency would become an even greater asset if professors of education regarded their own teaching as demonstrations of the content they present.

WHY TEACHERS FAIL

Teachers fail for many reasons, but inadequate knowledge of subject matter is seldom one of them. Numerous failures are to be expected in a profession numbering more than a million and a quarter practitioners. Unfortunately personal traits, defects of character, or a series of unhappy coincidences may cause failure. Excellent teachers may become involved in personality clashes that prevent effective direction of learning. At other times the fault has been one of adaptability, as in the case of one young man who could not adjust his urban attitudes to fit the rural area to which he had gone. Family obligations occasionally interfere with teaching duties. But despite all the claims that the teachers in today's schools do not know enough about their subjects, failure in teaching is rarely caused by lack of academic knowledge.

Most teachers who fail do so because they do not know *how to teach*. The most common cause of failure by far is the inability to guide students through a planned series of learning experiences. Teachers lack skill in the methods of teaching—precisely the skill that the professional courses in education were designed to develop. Teaching is complex and demanding. Those who have been trained for it acquire the art in different degrees, to be sure, and a few of them never become very proficient in the competencies they should have learned in their professional courses. They fail in teaching because they have failed in learning to teach.

Knowledge of subject matter is no assurance of successful teaching, because no one can guarantee any relationships between knowledge and teaching ability. Master teachers possess both; others have little of either. Those in between represent every combination of knowledge and teaching skill. A reasonable amount of each is essential—and adequate for most school situations, for not everyone can be expected to become a master teacher. Any number of subject matter specialists, including some who have had successful teaching records in colleges, have failed in the public schools because they were unable to control the learning activities of their students. The proposition that anyone who knows a subject can teach it is open to serious doubt.

TEACHING HAS FUNDAMENTALS TOO

A variant of the "knowledge alone is adequate preparation for teaching" view argues that an intelligent person acquires considerable understanding of teaching incidentally, in the course of his own education and from friends who are teachers. Very few similar statements have been made in the last half century about such professions as medicine and engineering, though no doubt a smattering of either can be obtained incidentally. Ironically, those who would favor the incidental learning of teaching are also uniformly and vehemently opposed to the theory that children can acquire fundamental skills incidentally through activities motivated by other interests. Unquestionably, many children do learn much about grammar and spelling from reading for pleasure, but both skills are also taught intensively in the schools. The incidental knowledge of how to teach must be similarly supplemented by systematic study in regular courses.

Teaching has an indispensable content of professional knowledge and skills that must be learned through disciplined study. The art has become so complex that the day of the "born teacher" is nearly over. Nor can teaching be learned satisfactorily "on the job." Even the beginning teacher is today expected to bring with him familiarity with innumerable details and techniques of his profession. The alternative to professional education for teaching is trial-and-error learning of its fundamentals at the expense of the students, and at the risk of an inevitably high percentage of failure.

Attempts to teach without a reasonable command of the fundamental skills of instruction are fumbling efforts in which students and subject content are coordinated only accidentally and occasionally. This type of faulty teaching is common, though not nearly as common now as it was a generation ago. It would occur much more frequently should the critics of the public schools ever succeed in destroying the design of professional teacher education, for which they have proposed no substitute. Indeed, they do not even discuss the skills of teaching in the extensive current criticisms of public education.

During the same postwar years in which professional teacher education has been criticized so vigorously, many college faculties have begun to examine the quality of their own teaching. Articles have been written and conferences held on the subject. Courses in methods of teaching have even been proposed for graduate students planning careers in higher education. Here then, while a few college professors are blasting away at methods courses for public school teachers, some of their colleagues are seriously urging methods courses for prospective college instructors. What an interesting antithesis!

14. Scapegoating the Public School

An actively expressed reliance on public education has long been a tradition in America. As a result, today's child experiences a curriculum studded with activities reflecting the public's demands of its schools. Once, the school had as its only function the teaching of book learning. Now, after acceding to a long parade of past requests that the schools "should do something about it," education has acquired a host of other responsibilities.

But many of the more recent calls upon educators and education have been not so much requests as attacks. Indeed, the public school has become the butt of various individual and group aggressions and the scapegoat for many of our most serious national problems. Year after year, for example, some American mothers drove their sons three blocks to the elementary school, and called for them at dismissal time. Yet when, early in World War II, a large percentage of young Americans failed to meet the physical requirements of the armed forces, it was our "modern" type of education that was somehow felt to be at fault. Similarly with the postwar increase in juvenile delinquency. The burden of blame for this, as for many other problems, was deposited on the doorstep of the school and, more particularly, its system of "progressive education."

The most recent occasion for using the public school as a scapegoat was the successful launching of the first Soviet satellite. Within hours after the announcement that Sputnik I was in orbit, the schools were the object of an orgy of recrimination. Somebody or something had to be the culprit. And almost immediately—even among prominent people who might have been expected to know better—this painful role was assigned to education. It was all the American schools' fault!

THE BARRAGE OF WORDS

The barrage of words following upon the launching of the first Soviet satellite was quickly taken up by the mass media. Unsolicited criticism came from all quarters, from commentators, novelists—even from officers in the armed forces. And the preponderant viewpoint was one of unqualified denunciation. Few critics found anything to praise in our public schools, and only rarely did any public figure speak or write with anything like objectivity about the problems of American education.

All of the stock phrases of folklore were fired in this simple-minded barrage against American education. The curriculum was criticized for its "softness." High schools were said to have been "downgraded." A few of the lighter secondary courses were widely publicized as typical of high school subject offerings (until it became known that only 2 or 3 percent of the students in but a small number of schools were actually enrolled in them). The cry of "anti-intellectualism" was frequently heard, and "progressive education" was excoriated over and over again. Falling back on the twin myths of fixed standards and uniform students, some critics called for more tests and more homework, while others urged "harder" discipline and absolute achievement levels. And, of course, teacher education came in for its full share of knocks.

A few critics, it is true, earned the gratitude of the teaching profession by attacking the problems of education, not the educators. They pointed to the teachers' low pay scales, their long and strenuous hours of work, their overcrowded classes, their inadequate buildings and equipment, and the record of public apathy to their problems. Yet such minority voices were scarcely audible. However cogent and well-documented their analyses, they were drowned out in the general, recriminatory roar.

GIANT-STRIDE REASONING

It is only natural for a university professor to feel that high-school graduates do not know enough when they enter the university. Teachers at all levels tend to disparage the schools from which their incoming students are recruited. In actual fact, however, particularly in regard to the alleged lack of preparedness of high school students in scientific and technical subjects, a great deal of such criticism is grossly unwarranted.

The preparation for careers in science and technology barely *begins* in the high school. A very much larger part is accomplished during the college and university years. For example, only a single year of chemistry and physics is taught in most high schools. At college, on the other hand, a student major in either of these subjects devotes at least thirty semester hours to its study, a matter of eight or ten separate courses. It is even possible for a student to begin chemistry and physics in college, and then to major in them, without having spent a single hour studying either of these sciences while at high school. How, then, can the fact that the United States was not the first country to orbit a satellite be attributed to our high schools? Would it not be considerably more plausible to say that it has been university science, if anything, whose adequacy has been put into question?

Yet certain officers in the armed services have leveled this type of unreasonable criticism against our high-school science offerings. What these people have forgotten is that it has not been our high schools that have been responsible for missile research and satellite development. These have necessarily been the proper business of our armed services, working with the massive resources of American science and technology. It is therefore hard to see how, save by reasoning in "giant strides," one can overlook the performance of our professional military men and scientists and address whatever complaints we may have about the American space program to our high schools.

How sadly out of contact professors and military men have in fact been with the actual situation in the nation's high schools may be seen in their persistent charge that our high-school students lack sufficient interest in science. Yet thousands of the students referred to have been busying themselves constructing home-made rockets, often with the help of their high-school science teachers, and their experiments have upon occasion been reported in the same magazine and newspaper

issues that elsewhere on their pages have carried the
solemn statements of the students' critics. The deter-
mination to keep attacking the schools is apparently so
strong that such reports have not even been noticed.

THE "LOOKY-LOOKY" EXAMPLES

One of the most popular scapegoating devices has
been the use of the single, isolated example as a basis
for statements claiming applicability to education as a
whole: "Once I observed a class . . ." "I know a student who . . ." "Let me tell you of a case in
which . . ." The observer's attention is directed to *one*
class, *one* student, *one* case, out of many.

As everyone knows, one can find examples to prove
almost anything. The "Looky Finger" can be pointed at
the time-wasting of an idle student, the frivolities of a
number of students and, upon occasion, even at such
seeming incongruities as a fifth-grade textbook being
used in an eighth-grade class. Yet such single examples
prove nothing—save that they exist and, in some cases
at least, probably exist for very good, if particular reasons. The eighth-graders using the fifth-grade textbook,
for instance, are in all likelihood comprised of the lowest 2 per cent in the school in their ability to read.

The schools in most American communities offer examples to fit all purposes. Every example that can be
cited may easily be matched by another proving its
very opposite. A few steps down the hall from the slow
class of eighth-graders is another of thirty-one seventh-
graders writing compositions that would do credit to
students at least three years farther along. The "fact"
that girls and boys of low ability seldom enroll in physics is balanced by the "fact" that most students with

high performance levels do take such courses. High-school registers include the names of juvenile delin-quents; Eagle Scouts are also listed. Only good judg-ment prevents choosing either as an example of the whole student body.

The art of choosing a true example presents the deli-cate problem of finding a single case which is truly rep-resentative of a larger number. It is possible for the description of an individual case to be factually com-plete and accurate and yet entirely false when cited as an example of other cases. A specific student or course must be typical of other students or courses, or it is not a true example. But to be both specific and typical is exceedingly difficult. A youth who ranks in the upper third of his class may be a good example of the bright student, but he cannot be typical of the entire school. Probably he is not really representative of all of the top third of his own class, for the youngsters included in it undoubtedly display many dissimilarities. Very likely no single individual can be typical of more than a certain type of student. Yet the example technique has actually been misused to label 24,000 American high schools by the "facts" about one student.

"IT MUST BE SO BECAUSE SO MANY PEOPLE ARE SAYING IT"

Constant and prominent repetition has convinced a part of the public that the charges against the American high school rest on facts. The remark has actually been made in a local PTA meeting that, "The high school must have been downgraded because so many people are saying so." Persons who have never had any con-tact with teacher education have come to PTA meet-ings prepared to deliver harangues against education courses. Others who have ripped into the "progressive education" in their local schools, live in communities whose schools are actually among the most conservative in the country. Firsthand acquaintance with the schools is rare; invariably these citizens quote from their reading, frequently without realizing that what they read was not based on actual knowledge either. The accepted preparation for anyone who wishes to comment on education seems to be the reading of one or two of the more sensational exposés. This satisfies the test of plausibility at least, for they are all very similar. The reader then becomes one more of those who have "made it true" by saying it. Only now and then does anyone try to acquaint himself with schools by visiting some classes; and who ever borrows a professional book or two from an educator friend?

The type of reasoning illustrated by the old proverb, "Where there's smoke, there must be fire," can lead quickly to the conclusion that the educational folklore, of which the bulk of current criticism is compounded, is the truth of the situation. It may be that the proverb will hold true when actual smoke is sighted, but it is a far cry from: "Where there's enough talk, there must be truth." Incidentally, the proverb does not specify that, in this case, the smoking fire burns most brightly in the eye of the critic.

SO MUCH CRITICISM FROM SO FEW

The great volume of denunciations of public education might lead to the inference that there were multitudes of critics busily turning out their pronouncements. But much the largest part of the fuss and furor has consisted of much-publicized quotations and paraphrases from a rather small number of persons—a handful of college professors, novelists, and admirals. It is conceivable that their sizzling comments have also increased the circulation of the periodicals in which they were featured. Their views echo and re-echo in the expressed opinions of many other individuals.

Apparently this vociferous group has gained wider credence across the nation than the 1,300,000 certificated professionals who staff the public schools. Such newsworthiness brings to mind the ritualistic question of a certain masculine society, "How gained you this recognition?" Some critics, of course, had already attained a measure of distinction, but others have basked in a new prominence created by their attacks upon education. It is a singular, but undeniable truth that it has become easier to build a popular reputation as an authority on education by criticizing the schools than by teaching in them. Persons who probably could not meet the certification requirements for teaching in any state have been read and heard in preference to hundreds of thousands of men and women who have followed life careers in education.

The surge into prominence of the clamorous few has been as spectacular as the sudden stardom of a motion-picture heroine. Vaulting over the usual arduous years of professional study and practice, they have become experts on education overnight. Once their reputations as critics have been established, their output of denunciation has continued to receive a wide hearing. Their success in obtaining audiences is a peculiar verification of the old saying, "There's always room at the top."

TEN YEARS BEHIND THE TIMES

Although the improvement of learning in high-school subjects is always a concern of teachers and administrators, more than the usual interest in strengthening the mathematics and science courses began to appear at the end of World War II. By 1948 or 1949, interest had become sufficiently noticeable to be regarded as a definite trend in secondary education. It was quite apparent to the professionals that the drift (begun in the 1930's) away from these courses had ceased, and that new appreciation of their importance had developed.

Impetus for the awakening of interest in mathematics and science came from several sources. The demands of modern warfare undoubtedly were influential factors, as was the United States' leadership in nuclear fission. Perhaps even more important was the nation's need for technicians, scientists, and engineers in the expanding postwar industrial technology—in contrast to the economic depression of the previous decade when employment opportunities were too few to absorb all of the trained personnel. Education in the United States has always been a means of improving social and economic status, and the postwar rewards for scientific and technical education have been powerful incentives for youth.

But for several years, the trend toward science and mathematics was known almost exclusively by the schools themselves. It was publicized so little that it was practically unnoticed elsewhere. But it continued to gain momentum into the 1950's. More teachers and counselors began to advise their able students to take the advanced courses in science and mathematics, and principals began to include such paragraphs as the following in their spring preregistration bulletins to students and parents:

> As far as can now be foreseen, employment opportunities will be excellent for persons with scientific and technical education. The foundation for these careers begins in the advanced science and mathematics courses in the high school. Students who have the abilities and the interests to profit from them are urged to register for these subjects.

The qualified recommendation to "students who have the abilities and interests to profit" is an indication of understanding in educational planning. No effort was made to persuade all students to take chemistry and trigonometry, nor was alarm manifested over whatever percentage of students registered for these and other academic subjects. The actual and appropriate concern was that youngsters take the courses which best matched their own capacities and aptitudes. It would seem reasonable today to expect anyone who writes about mathematics and science teaching to exhibit some knowledge of this trend. The movement to re-emphasize the high-school science and mathematics courses has been ignored by public education's most acrimonious critics—clear evidence that none of them is very well acquainted with the schools they have censured so frequently and so severely. Their criticisms would have been much more timely fifteen years ago when their complaints about lack of interest and small enrollments in the mathematics and science courses could have earned them places among the leaders in secondary education. Now their statements reveal ignorance of a trend that has been well under way for more than ten years.

The Advanced Placement Program, described in Chapter X, in which hundreds of American secondary schools participate, is another factor that has been ignored by the critics of education. It has been designed to enable high schools to offer to selected students courses equivalent to those taught in the first year of college. These advanced courses can be publicized as easily as those of lighter nature which have been played up so extensively, particularly when American and European secondary education are compared.

Most of the recent popular treatments of the American high school read as though they were planned to create an image of education without substance or depth. It should be heartening to learn that thousands of high-school seniors are doing excellent work in subjects previously taught only at the college level, receiving advanced standing in the colleges in mathematics, science, English, history, and foreign languages. It might be interesting to speculate whether certain of the high-school's critics have not known of the Advanced Placement Program or have not cared to mention it.

WHO DESIGNED THE SATELLITES?

Denunciators of public education credited the design and production of the first Sputnik to the efficiency of Russian education. Innumerable comparisons of American and Russian secondary education were made for public consumption. Most of them stressed the concentration on mathematics and science in Russian education, implying that this emphasis had enabled Russia to establish superiority in missile research and production. The statements that the Russians were ahead of us, and that their youth were required to study more mathematics and science, were linked together repeatedly as though the second situation was the cause of the first, the inference being that the satellites were the direct products of contemporary secondary education.

But secondary-school studies do not lead quite so quickly to such complex, advanced results. In between are many years of undergraduate and graduate specialization and a good many more of experience. It should be evident to everyone that the satellites represent the combined efforts of many mature scientists whose secondary education almost certainly was received before 1940, probably even before 1930. Assuming the normal age of eighteen for high school graduation, an American scientist who was forty-five in 1958 would have attended high school from 1927 to 1931. Comparisons between the Soviet and American educational systems for the twenty years from 1920 to 1940 would thus have been more pertinent to the success of the satellites but such contrasts were not to be found in the tumultuous post-satellite scapegoating of the public schools.

Stories about German scientists who have contributed to the development of the United States' satellites have also been prominent in the news. Although their efforts have not been publicized as widely, other Germans have worked similarly for Russia. These men received their education in pre-World War II Germany, and their early experience was in the wartime development of that country's long-range rockets. Their recent work, whether in the United States or Russia, reflects nothing at all of the quality of secondary education in either country at the present time. When the facts are studied, any other relationships between current secondary education and the production of the satellites are equally improbable.

THE SCHOOLS' GREATEST NEED

The greatest need of the American public schools at the present time is financial support. The real deficiencies in public education—insufficient supply of qualified teachers, overcrowded classes and buildings, and shortages of equipment—can only be corrected by larger expenditures of money. The inadequacies of teachers' salaries have been made very clear by the exodus of teachers from the profession and the failure to attract able young people to fill the natural vacancies due to death and retirement. In spite of all of the publicity about the meagerness of teachers' salaries, there has been no widespread trend to correct this situation. In most communities, frequent, but small, accretions have barely kept pace with rises in costs of living. Large increases are badly needed in order to attract more students to the profession. The prestige of teaching suffers more from the frugal standard of living endured by teachers than from any other factor. The teacher's salary is satisfactory when it is the second income in the household, but it is not adequate to carry the entire burden of family expenses.

Teaching loads, never light, have everywhere become excessive as the public schools' responsibilities have been augmented by a host of tasks other than instruction. Most schools urgently need additions of at least 20 per cent to their present faculties. This would enable administrators to arrange reasonable teaching schedules, making work loads comparable to those in other occupations with which teaching must compete for personnel. Increases in both salaries and numbers of teachers will be expensive, but surely the price is small compared to the dividend of high-quality education.

Overcrowding is almost always a local problem which can be relieved only by the willingness of a majority of local residents to raise their taxes. Except in rare cases in which federal government enterprises have been responsible for sudden increases in enrollment, and federal funds have been granted to the local schools, each community must manage the construction of its own school buildings and employ enough teachers to staff them. Like teachers' salaries, the numbers of students in classes and buildings are measures of a community's ability and readiness to support the education of its children.

THE REAL CRISIS IN EDUCATION

The real crisis in American education is the meagerness of resources that forces the professionals in most public schools to operate at levels of efficiency below those of which they are capable. Educators can agree with their critics that the general situation is growing worse, but it is not, as so many of public education's detractors have argued, a crisis of knowledge and methods; it is a crisis of financial support. Few teachers today are able to teach as well as they know how. Far too many are "teaching on the run" because of handicaps in work loads and facilities. Their opportunities to complete professional tasks to their individual satisfactions are cut short by the pressure of innumerable other duties. Everyone today is aware of the tremendous growth in school enrollments since World War II, but very few realize that the teacher's job has expanded as well. Teachers are now expected to do a great deal more for each one of at least as many students as they had in earlier years. The resulting inability to "get around to" all of their many tasks has been accumulating steadily for many years. Too much to do, with too little time and resources, is the real crisis.

The fact that so many teachers everywhere have stuck it out despite their daily frustrations and the increasing attractiveness of other occupations is a working monument to the quality of their professional education and ethics. Their solid and splendid accomplishments have created and maintained the finest public schools in the world. These hardworking professionals are the greatest resources of those schools.

DOES SCAPEGOATING SIGNIFY TRUE CONCERN?

If the clamor of criticism is an indication of genuine concern for the quality of American education, the logical result should be much larger school budgets. The fact that the American people can afford anything they are convinced they need, and a good many luxuries as well, has been demonstrated repeatedly. The key question is whether the current alarm is genuine enough to convince people that improvement of the schools is really necessary.

But it is entirely possible that the scapegoating of public education by a few persons, and ready acceptance of it by so many others, is a symptom of mass evasion of responsibility. Perhaps the national excitement generated by the news of Sputnik I is to be dissipated in scapegoating rather than translated into serious efforts to raise the material standards of education. The keenness of the wish to do something in a crisis can be dulled as readily by casting blame about as by constructive endeavors to improve the situation from which the crisis emerged. Faultfinding is certainly less expensive in the short run than constructing, equipping, and staffing good schools, even though eventually it may prove to be the most costly bargain the nation has ever known. The quality of American education already suffers far more from lack of money than from all the mythical faults attributed to it by folklore.

The real test of meaning of the unprecedented publicity for education lies just ahead, in the public's willingness to allot larger portions of their incomes for the operation of the public schools. Within the next few years, referenda on the construction of new buildings will be held in hundreds of American communities. Local boards of education will be petitioned annually to raise the levels of their teachers' salaries. If both of these requests for additional funds are approved throughout the country, it is fair to conclude that most of the expressed concern for education has been genuine. Wholesale failure to gain approval will indicate beyond doubt that the scapegoating has been a substitute for action.

Public education in the United States has been one of the greatest and most successful human experiments ever attempted. It now faces serious questioning of its motives and its capacities. The near future will be crucial in shaping the role the public schools are to have in American life.

15. Who Shall Decide?

The folklore of education flourishes because of two characteristics of the American culture, both of which have been described in earlier chapters. One is the effect of complex factors such as occupational specialization, which has separated the activities of teachers so completely from those of other adults. Parents turn over the education of their children to a school which most of them never see in the full scope of its operations. They depend upon the teachers for instruction as the teachers depend upon the parents to support the school and to supply a host of personal and family needs. The other characteristic is the increasingly rapid rate of change in education itself. No longer can parents take for granted that their children's instruction is identical to that which they received in the same grade at the same age.

Lack of first-hand knowledge of education places parents in an awkward position. They are susceptible to accounts of education which appear in the great modern means of mass communication; seldom do they have the close and exact knowledge necessary to evaluate all that they see, hear, and read about the schools. Folklore can be as plausible and convincing as the facts to persons who are unacquainted with prevailing practices. The extent to which parents regularly receive their information about the public schools from extraneous sources is illustrated by the plans of the school officials of one large American city to place a feature article describing important aspects of the curriculum in a magazine of national circulation so that parents could read about them there. Surely the necessity of such a procedure confirms the outright separation of the schools from adult life.

EDUCATION AS THE SUBJECT OF STUDY

A return to the school is urgently needed in the form of a massive program designed to acquaint adults with the real curriculum provided for their children. It will be most unfortunate if the American people permit themselves to remain uninformed about events as crucial to them as the education they support and upon which their survival so importantly depends. The future of any nation, and of its citizens individually, is inseparable from the quality of public education. No modern culture could survive for more than a generation without the benefits of an uninterrupted flow of young, newly educated designers, producers, and consumers. Moreover, the education of each generation must be improved in both efficiency and quality to enable citizens to cope with the problems of an increasingly complex civilization. To make intelligently the major decisions about public education which are their ultimate responsibility, citizens need to know more about school procedures.

The operations of the public schools should become part of the subject matter of public education. Children should begin to learn *about* the schools while they are *in* the schools, and should continue to learn as adults. Some beginnings in instruction about the schools have already been made. For example, it is quite common to include in the seventh-grade curriculum some materials on orientation to the junior high school. A large number of senior high schools schedule time for the orientation of their new students. This type of instruction might well begin in the elementary grades. The incidental knowledge of public education which children acquire in their academic progress is useful, but it is often inaccurate and incomplete. Courses teaching about the schools can correct both of these weaknesses.

Education about the schools should be planned to continue through adulthood, but the formal methods of teaching appropriate for children would have little value. Few adults can be expected to attend regularly any sort of classlike program even though the content deals with their own children. Somewhat more effective would be the sort of flexible activities that have been developed for use in adult education courses: forums, panel presentations, small group discussions, as well as occasional lectures by appropriate specialists. A continuing sequence of such activities might well develop from some of the programs which are now arranged for PTA's and other community organizations. For individual study of the schools, reading is the best way adults can keep themselves informed. An impressive quantity of educational comment for the lay reader has already been published in books and periodicals. Its volume is increasing, and will continue to increase in response to the current interest in the public schools.

Yet the means of study suggested above can promise only limited results. They will require more sustained motivation than most of today's busy adults are likely to bring to the task. Hence the schools must also devise various other methods of keeping the public informed of their operations. Perhaps printed materials can be developed to be sent home with children and mailed to nonparents. For example, an illustrated brochure might describe the science program in the elementary school. It could include the topics of science, the amount of class time, the expectations of homework, the kinds of equipment used, the learning activities, and the special projects to be completed for each grade. Problems of teaching science at these levels might well be treated also. Another school system might prefer to encompass the entire science curriculum through the senior high school in a single brochure. Any of the school subjects, or a service area such as guidance, could be presented in the same manner. Revisions from time to time, as changes were made in the curriculum, would keep such printed materials up-to-date. The dissemination of information would enable parents to follow the education of their children as closely as they wished. Such a program would eliminate current misunderstandings, and immunize a large section of the public against unfounded criticisms of the public schools.

BUILDING UNDERSTANDING AND CONCERN

A lively and continuing adult interest in public education offers the best possible means of dispelling the shreds of folklore which now obscure the public's understanding of the operations of their schools. General comprehension of the vast differences among children's opportunities and abilities in our culture will prevent us from comparing average American high-school students with the highly selected 5 percent in a European secondary school. At the same time, valid comparisons of the most capable students from both will be appropriate as a useful source of mutual improvement. Similarly, the myths of fixed standards and uniform students will be replaced by concern for a sufficiently differentiated curriculum to serve the multitudinous educational needs of the real children and youth who attend the public schools. At least some of the complaints about discipline will disappear as citizens submit themselves to the discipline of the facts about the schools. But the most satisfactory result of all will be *accurate* criticism of educational programs instead of the current flurry of excitement in which a local school system may find itself advised from prominent sources to begin the teaching of certain subject matter which has been in its curriculum for a decade or even more.

Public concern to learn more about the schools will be welcomed by educators and members of local boards of education who have wrestled with the problems of effectively communicating the facts about the schools. Most of them would be gratified should the curriculum come to rival the extracurricular program as a source of local news. In the same way, as teachers see public interest grow in their innovations in teaching, their already fine efforts will be intensified. Furthermore, greater understanding of the demands modern education places upon the teacher can hardly fail to enhance the prestige of the profession.

THE REAL TASKS OF AMERICAN EDUCATION

The real tasks of American education are truly formidable. They are also well known to everyone who has studied the schools by observing them and reading the professional literature. These stubborn, harassing tasks, which the educator cannot escape as easily as his critics, are those of matching learning experiences to the individual needs and abilities of all pupils. The results of hundreds of serious studies of the problems of American education have made unmistakably clear the fundamental inaccuracy of any conception of public education which does not include the need for individual and group differentiation. The foremost task of the public school must be defined as that of being many schools at one and the same time.

The educational task would be greatly simplified if it could be limited to the teaching of a maximum amount of subject matter to the children most able to absorb it. This is the function of education which has been implied most frequently in the recent series of attacks upon the public schools. It would convert public education into a twelve-year cram for an intellectual elite whose number would diminish year by year as those who were unable to maintain the pace were eliminated. Undoubtedly, those who survived would be exceedingly well prepared for college. Expenditures for public education would be much less than they are now, for great savings could be effected by offering fewer services for smaller numbers of children. The reduced numbers of students would also result in enormous savings in higher education. Probably a large number of colleges could be closed down.

But the greatest achievements of American mass education would be sacrificed. The anticipated advantages would prove to be largely imaginary. Any gain in college preparation would not be large, for the highest ranking high-school graduates make excellent college records under the present multipurpose system of public education. The uniquely American development of public education for *all* would disappear with the elimination of such essential features as the exploratory function of the junior high school and the vocational, technical, commercial, and general curricula of the senior high school. Logic would also dictate the abandonment of remedial instruction in such tool subjects as reading and arithmetic, for the elite would not need it, and the others would not remain in the school long enough to benefit from it. Increases in the number of retarded children in each of the elementary grades would result from higher rates of failure. Probably most of the children of the ages which are now considered normal for junior high school would still be struggling in the elementary school, for the highly selective nature of the program would necessitate annual failure for the majority, who would find the school a bleak and dismal experience.

At the present time, the only situations in which sole attention can be given to an elite group of highly selected students are in the specialized high schools of a very few, very large American cities. In these metropolitan centers such high schools are but one phase of the whole secondary program which also includes general high schools as well as others with different specialties. At the other extreme of secondary education are the tiny high schools, with enrollments of less than one hundred students, which still survive in the most rural sections of the country. Their meager resources and small faculties limit their curricula to a bare minimum of the most easily presented college preparatory subjects which are really appropriate for only a minority of their students. The most nearly typical American high schools do reasonably well in providing education for *all* of the community's youth by offering a comprehensive program, including the academic, under one roof.

Multipurpose mass education is not the invention of the American educator. His role has been chiefly that of guiding its development in response to public demands for more and more variety in the school program. By implication, at least, the public has rejected the idea of education only for the elite with each addition to the curriculum which originally comprised only the fundamentals in the elementary school and the classical subjects in the secondary school. These were, and still are, the studies regarded as most appropriate for the exceptionally able, an opinion to which a good number of educators would take some exception. The American people have sent all of their children to school, they have demanded curricular variety to suit the many purposes and capacities of their children, and they have taxed themselves to support this type of school. Educational leadership has done its part in organizing the public schools to satisfy the expressed wishes of the public.

DIFFERENTIATION SHOULD CONTINUE

It will be necessary for the schools to continue to plan subject materials and methods of instruction to serve differences in individual capacities and aims. Indeed, the organization of the multipurpose curriculum has barely passed through the earliest stages of its development. Much is still to be learned, and much remains to be done, about the twin problems of arranging sufficient variety and flexibility to accommodate the complete ranges of purposes and abilities of students who represent the entire population. Neither materials nor methods are as yet adequate to satisfy the known needs of all who attend the schools.

MORE ATTENTION FOR THE MORE ABLE

Because the problems of the most able students are especially prominent at this time, it is probable that these youngsters will receive more attention in the near future than any other segment of the school population. The quickening of trends in both acceleration and enrichment, which are already well established, is a certainty. Here, as in so many other instances, educational planning will respond to the demands of the public. The addition of advanced courses designed for the brightest youth should be anticipated in the senior high school as one phase of the effort, and the number of star sections in the present courses should also be expected to increase. The introduction of the most talented students to the great academic disciplines is likely to move down the educational ladder by a year, or even two. Elementary algebra, for example, which has been taught universally in the ninth grade, may be expected in the eighth grade, or even the seventh, for selected classes, which will have had a prior year or two of accelerated arithmetic. The probabilities are that all of the devices designed to aid the superior student which were described in Chapter X will come into even more general usage.

The educational needs of the remainder of the school population are in no way less deserving of effort because they have been temporarily eclipsed by the sudden eminence of the intellectually talented, whom they far outnumber. Students on the middle and lower planes of academic ability are just as unique and precious as individuals as their brighter contemporaries, and their education merits the same high quality of planning and teaching. The problems of their learning will remain under study. Improvements in both teaching materials and methods designed specifically for them should result in more efficient adaptations of the rate and scope of their learnings to their capacities.

THE MULTITRACK CURRICULUM

Some subjects, such as English and the social studies, will bear the same labels for all students, but the rate and intensity with which the materials are covered will vary with the ability of the classes. Eleventh-grade English, for instance, probably will be offered on anywhere from two to six levels, depending upon the size of the high school and the composition of the student body. The lowest will be somewhat below the equivalent of some ninth-grade English courses, while the highest will surpass much of the work now done in the first two years of college. This will not be wholly new, for such differentiations are in effect in several hundred high schools at the present time, where they are usually designated as programs of two tracks, three tracks, etc. However, the multitrack curriculum should become more common, and improvements in the efficiency of instruction at each level can be anticipated as reasonable outcomes of the expansion.

Some of the other courses cannot be planned on as many levels because of their abstractness and difficulty. Chemistry and physics, for example, could only be taught on the upper tracks of a multitrack curriculum. Attempts to adapt these subjects for simpler presentations would result only in the repetition of portions of the general science courses in the junior high school. The advanced mathematics courses are similar in their inherent limitations upon simplification. Students who have shown no evidence of ability to profit from the study of abstract science and mathematics will continue to be advised to elect other subjects in which their success is more probable. In some cases the choice of other subjects will be made because of individual purposes instead of abilities.

The strong probability of an increase in the number of multitrack curricula does not indicate universal agreement among educators that this sort of program is the best means of dealing with individual and group differences among students. The multitrack program puts into practice the principle of grouping students in classes according to abilities and achievements. Whether this should be done in the public schools has been the topic of a spirited controversy among educators for several decades. The presence of the multitrack curriculum in a school is evidence that the problems of serving different educational needs have been recognized and that serious attempts to solve them have been made. The disapproval in many other quarters illustrates the heterogeneity of American public education, a diversity in which schools have sought improvement in different ways.

Adaptations of the curriculum to satisfy student purposes and abilities have been in progress for several decades. The pace has been accelerated in recent years as more knowledge has been accumulated of students and methods of teaching subjects to them, but it is an acceleration of an established trend. Any proposals of curricular differentiation as a *new* remedy for the problems of public education reveal a woeful lack of knowledge of the operations of the public schools. It is long past the proper time for the public to realize that their schools have made a great deal more progress than the critics of education are willing to concede.

INTELLIGENCE AND INTEGRITY

The great preponderance of the adults who comprise the professional staff of the public schools are both intelligent and honest. Although it has not always been so regarded, teaching is primarily an intellectual activity which is neither inviting nor endurable to the unintelligent. Not all teachers can be ranked among the highest in intellectual ability, but the profession has attracted an impressive number of high-school and college honor students, and the average levels of intelligence are more than adequate to meet the demands of public school instruction. Moreover, teaching is a profession in which the display of intelligence is uniformly solicited and respected.

Teaching is also one of the most moral of occupations. This is expected by those who choose to enter the profession and by those who employ them. Public censure is quick and usually harsh for the minute percentage of teachers who violate the moral code of the community, but it is so rarely occasioned that it makes news because of its very incongruity. Parents demonstrate their confidence daily as they entrust to the teachers the responsibility for more than 37,000,000 children and youth.

It should be unnecessary to defend either the intelligence or the honesty of the educational profession were it not for the repeated insinuations that educators are responsible for a wholesale deterioration of public education in the United States. Some of the critics of the public schools have expressed freely their beliefs that teachers have deliberately debased the quality of education. Other critics have implied that teachers were unaware of the problems and needs of education. Earlier chapters have presented the case that the charges of deterioration are based entirely on folklore. The falsity of the accusations of ignorance and willful impairment can also be demonstrated.

THE PROFESSIONAL STUDY OF EDUCATION

Individually and in their professional organizations, teachers have studied the problems of education since the origin of the public schools. If anything is completely certain in the present world of change, it is the fact that teachers are aware of the difficulties that confront them. It is highly improbable that any critic of the public schools can discover any educational problem (or suggest a solution for it) that has not been investigated and reported in the professional literature of education.

Education has participated vigorously and effectively

in the "organizational revolution" of the last hundred years. Every teaching field in the specialized curriculum of the secondary school has long had its own national association. Elementary school organizations are also large and active. Other national groups are engaged in the more general study of the curriculum. Each of the professional specializations associated with teaching, such as guidance and the several areas of administration, also has a national organization. State, county, and local affiliations of the national associations are numerous. A tremendous volume of information is published and distributed in the forms of magazines, yearbooks, newsletters, and pamphlets.

A large number of books about education is published annually by individuals, in addition to the materials which are produced by the professional organizations. They cover every phase of public education. Several thousands of master's and doctor's theses are also completed each year in the graduate schools of education. Each reports the thorough investigation of a professional problem.

The nation's teachers have not been asleep, either before or during the present excitement over public education. The records of their concern and of their progress can be read in their literature and observed in their schools. It is not only extremely interesting, but also helps to verify this and the preceding paragraphs, that the best proposals to emerge from the current criticism of education so strongly reflect the best contemporary practices in the schools. Moreover, these proposals have been made by men who have observed and studied the actual situations in the schools, men who acknowledge that one of the major sources of their proposals has been the good work they have seen. They have written in the spirit of, "This is good. Let us have more of it." In contrast, the critics who apparently have neither observed nor read can only propose that the schools now abandon the progress of the last sixty years and return to programs which were even then inadequate.

The most valuable result that could be hoped for from the publicity education has received since the news of the first satellite is the firm and general resolution of the public to support their schools more strongly and understand them more thoroughly than ever before. It will be most fortunate if public concern has become sufficiently acute to generate vigorous local efforts to improve the public schools. Both the general and specific weaknesses of American education are well known among the profession, and real progress has been made toward their amelioration. Much more rapid advances can be made, however, with more generous support and understanding.

The greatest limitation upon improvement in the present school system has been shown to be financial. Lack of funds causes numerous specific weaknesses as a result of which school people are less effective than they know how to be. Although they are not identical for all communities, these weaknesses do exhibit some general similarities. In a great number of American school districts, more classrooms are needed to relieve double sessions and to permit the scheduling of smaller classes. Another specific and serious weakness is excessive teacher loads of too many and too large classes in which children cannot benefit from being known and treated as individuals. Specialized guidance personnel are too sparse in most school systems to be able to render the valuable services of which they are capable. They are more likely at present to be responsible for the advisement of 1,000 or more students, some four times as many as they should ideally be handling.

None of these weaknesses are of the sort which can be alleviated by denunciations of the professional educator. If an improvement in the teaching of fundamentals is really desired, more improvement can be made by reducing class sizes to the manageable number of twenty-five pupils than by scolding "progressive education" while packing thirty-eight or forty children into one old-fashioned classroom. The prevalent and proper solicitude for the welfare of the brighter students will also realize better results by reductions in the number of students per teacher. Where "gifted" pupils are now overlooked, as has so often been charged, the most probable reason is the large numbers of other children by whom they are surrounded.

Full realization of any complex problem comes slowly to most persons. It may be still too soon to hope that the American people have developed an understanding of the truly massive problems of educating all of their children. Yet without that understanding it is certainly too much to expect them either to contribute as amply as the scope of the problem necessitates, or to escape the basic inaccuracies of the folklore and scapegoating with which they have been deluged. We can only hope that understanding and support will grow together, and that each will enhance the other.

LOCAL DECISIONS FOR LOCAL SCHOOLS

The American way of making decisions about public schools has followed the principle of local choice within broad limits set by the state. Within these limits communities have had a great deal of freedom in the organization and operation of their schools. For the most part, state regulation of local schools has been exercised through the establishment of minimum standards. Every community has had the privilege of going as far beyond these standards as its citizens desire. In illustration, consider a state which requires that teachers have at least the bachelor's degree and twenty semester hours of education courses; that they be paid not less than $4,000 per year; that the schools operate for at least 170 days of at least six hours each; and that every high-school graduate must have earned a minimum of sixteen units of credit. Nothing in these regulations prevents a local school system from employing teachers with master's or doctor's degrees; from paying them on a schedule with maximum salaries of $9,000; from holding seven-hour sessions for 190 days; or from awarding diplomas to students who have been required to complete eighteen units of high-school credit.

The American way of planning schools has followed the leadership of professional educators, usually acting upon their recommendations, but with complete freedom to reject them, a freedom which has been exercised on innumerable occasions. Every major change in a school system, as well as most minor alterations, has been made only with the approval of a local board of education. The adoption of new textbooks and the addition of new subjects to the curriculum, for example, are matters which are nearly always subject to board approval. Decisions which involve the expenditure of large sums are regularly submitted to the people of the community. The erection of new school buildings in most communities requires a majority vote at a special election, and the annual school budget usually cannot be approved until after public hearings have been held. In recent years, solicitation of community opinion has fostered the organization of groups of lay citizens to study school problems. Professional leadership, controlled by local judgment, has designed and directed the American system of public education.

THE CHALLENGE TO PROFESSIONAL LEADERSHIP

This procedure of making decisions is now under challenge. The challenges are contained in every denunciation of professional educators and every demand for central controls over local education. Attacks upon the educators' qualifications and judgments are direct challenges to their present functions of leadership in local school districts. When school people are scapegoated for the country's position in the international missile race, as has happened so often lately, both their judgment in making recommendations and the community's judgment in accepting them are challenged. Both kinds of judgment are similarly questioned in other proposals which seek to take decisions out of local hands. One such proposal would create a national system of examinations; another offers a plan for the sudden reorganization of the high-school curriculum; a third would attempt a huge evaluation of the training of the nation's teachers. Not only do these proposals ignore sound present efforts, but all carry the clear implication

of inadequacy on the part of local boards of education
and the professionals they have employed to staff their
schools. In the respect of conveying criticism indirectly
while seeming to offer assistance, the proposals are
adroit refinements in the art of scapegoating.

THE PRESENT ALTERNATIVES

The present organization of the public schools places
them under the direction of qualified men and women
who have made their careers in education. These are
the professional educators. Their opinions on educational problems are proposed as specific, local recommendations which are dependent upon local citizens for
approval. The new alternatives would substitute decisions made by men and women whose careers have
not been in professional education. These are the critics
of the schools, some of whom are making new careers
for themselves as professional snipers at public education. To date, they have shown no inclination to con-
sult the opinions of parents and taxpayers on their
proposals for changes in the schools. Their propositions
have been expressed in the most general terms with little or no reference to specific school systems.

The choice of whose recommendations to follow will
be made sooner or later by the American people. Much
more than the simple choice between recommendations
will be involved, however. If the judgment of professional educators continues to be followed, the present
system of locally administered schools for all of the
nation's children will be maintained. The educational
needs of children of all levels of ability will receive
equal concern. Changes in public education will be
made in accordance with definite knowledge of Ameri-

can children and communities. Probably the rate of change will be accelerated, for the amount of such knowledge is growing rapidly, and communication among the members of the profession is becoming more effective. Most of the changes are likely to be further refinements of the established trends to differentiate and enrich instruction.

The alternative to professional leadership would substitute nationally controlled uniformity for differentiation, and folklore for knowledge. The statements of the leading spokesmen of this position have made it clear beyond any doubt that an inflexible type of educational program would be planned for the most intellectual students with little attention to the abilities and hopes of the majority of children. The advocates of such a program have no educational theory of their own. The best of their proposals have been borrowed from good present practices, and so can add nothing to what has been developed by the educators. The rest of their remarks are no more than general expressions of discontent with things as they are. Their opposition to much of the present curriculum has been characterized by folklore and distortion. It has been dominated by statements of what they are against, with scanty details of what they are "for." Their sweeping recommendations have not been accompanied by specific plans of what is to be taught or who is to teach it. Not one has presented anything as concrete as a course of study for even a single subject. The result of following their recommendations could only be a public-school system that served the educational needs of very few of the public's children.

Public education in the United States has many serious problems, of which the professionals are fully

aware, and on which effective efforts are being ex-
pended. The long record of improvement in the public
schools has barely been scanned by critics who now
propose to abandon successful programs, presumably to
initiate gigantic plans of reconstruction according to
their own notions of the purposes and methods of
education. The professional educator would be the first
to admit that his programs are still imperfect and incomplete. But the remedy is not to forsake sound programs because they have not yet reached the ultimate
in effectiveness. The most valuable criticism anyone can
offer public education is that which is based upon solid
understanding of present curricula and which proposes
feasible improvements in them. A steady and abundant
stream of this kind of criticism flows from within the
educational profession at all times. It is less effective
than could be wished because the public schools lack
funds. It is for this reason that so many schools everywhere today lag behind the best of known practices.
The road to better schools is unmistakably clear. Further
improvement in public education requires only public
confidence and public support.

Index

Acceleration, 198-201, 284
Achievement, 33
Achievement tests, 34, 42, 44, 161, 175-177
Adjustment, 235
Advanced Placement Program, 198-200
Aggression, 62-64, 68
Agricultural curriculum, 158, 168
Agriculture, 163
Agriculture, vocational, 215
Aid to parochial schools, 119-120
Aid to segregated schools, 119-120
Algebra, advanced, 160
Algebra, elementary, 19, 158, 160, 210, 284
Algebra, intermediate, 160, 210
American history, 23, 212
Analytics, 158
Ancient history, 186
Apprentice, village, 95-97
Aptitude tests, 161
Arithmetic, 42
Art, 163

Associations, educational, 289
Athletics, 55-56, 131, 162, 196, 214
Authoritarian teacher, 76

Baby-sitter, 97-99
Biology, 22, 210
Black Beauty, 99
Bookkeeping, 159, 160
Bookkeeping curriculum, 160
Books, expense to parents, 129-130
Brownies, 36
Business arithmetic, 158-159, 160
Business machines, 159, 160

Calculus, 158
California Achievement Test, 34
Campers Club, 162
Certification of teachers, emergency, 102, 187-188, 244
Changes in American life, 147-148
Changing tax structures, 111

Chemistry, 160, 209, 210, 211, 213, 262-263, 286
Class ring, expense to parents, 134
Clubs, 162
College Entrance Examination Board, 199
College entrance examinations, 187
College influence on high school, 150-153
College preparatory curriculum, 158, 160
Combinations of ability and opportunity, 46-48
Commercial Club, 162
Commercial curriculum, 158, 160, 168, 215
Commercial subjects, 163
Common learnings, 166
Competition and cooperation in the school, 53-56
Complex and simple answers, 9-11
Cooperative decision making, 230-233
Core curriculum, 166, 167
Costs of education, 104-105, 108, 129-134, 151, 162, 163, 164, 196
Course of study, 57-58
Cowboys, 220
Crane, Stephen, 21
Credit, recorded in units, 151-152
Crisis in education, 273-274
Cub Scouts, 35
Cumulative record, 191-192
Curricula, 158, 160, 168, 212, 215, 216

Debate on education, 1, 16, 17
Dedicated teacher, 88-92
Deerslayer, 21
Demonstration Guidance Project, 45
Departmentalized secondary school, 164-167, 198-199
Differences in achievement, 42
Differences in communities' abilities to finance schools, 105-107
Differentiated curriculum, 157-161
Difficult subjects, 208-211
Doctor's degree, 247
Dramatics, expense to parents, 131-132
Driver education, 163
Dropouts, 124, 135-136, 139, 202-203

Eagle Scouts, 265
Early school leavers, 124, 135-136, 139, 202-203
Economic self-sufficiency, 234
Economics, 160
Education as a science, 8-9
Education courses for the secondary teacher, 246
Educational associations, 289
Educational psychology, 246
Egghead, 221
Electives, 208, 209
Elementary algebra, 19, 158, 160, 210, 284
Elementary teachers' education, 247-248
Emergency care, 36
Emergency certification, 102, 187-188, 244

Emerson, 220

Eminence, Professor, 248

Employment, part-time, 83-84, 132, 168-169

English, 155-156, 160, 218

Enrichment, 284

Experience and interest, 48-51

Exportation of education, 110-111, 116, 122-123

Extra-curricular activities, 131-132, 137-138, 162-163

Family buying practices, 128

Family, educational expectations, 13, 136, 161

Family income, 128

Federal aid to education, 112-118

Feingold, S. Norman, 202

Film library, 239

Film strips, 239

Financial Aid for College Students, 202

Folklore in employment, 31-32

Foreign Language Club, 162

Foreign languages, 78-79, 166

French National Honor Society, 198

Fringe area, 107

Frustration, 62, 64, 73, 80, 89

General business, 160

General curriculum, 158, 160, 168

General Educational Development Test, 32

General mathematics, 159, 160

General methods of teaching, 246

General science, 160

Geometry, plane, 160, 210

Geometry, solid, 158, 160, 210

German scientists, 271

Giant stride reasoning, 262-264

Good Old Days, 6-7, 33, 86, 168

Golden Age, 6-7, 228

Graduation, expense to parents, 133

Graduation, requirements, 212-213

Great Debate on Education, 1, 16, 17

Greek, 186

Guidance, 246

Guidance folder, 191-192

Habitual offenders, 67-68

Hamlet, 21

Health, 160

Health program, 36

Health records, 36

High school enrollment, 146-147

Homemaking, 163, 215

Homemaking curriculum, 158

Honor Roll, 197, 204

Honor societies, 198

Hot lunch program, 119

Identification of bright children, 191-192

Immunization, 36

Incident and process, 75-76

Incidental learnings, 258

Inconstant subject, 18-21

Incorrigibles, 69-70

Individual folder, 191-192

Industrial arts, 160

Integration of subjects, 19

Intelligence quotient, 34

Intelligence tests, 161
Intermediate algebra, 160, 210
Interscholastic athletics, 55-56, 131, 162, 196, 214
Iowa Achievement Test, 34
IQ, 200
Itinerant pedagogue, 92-95
Ivanhoe, 21

Junior high school scheduling practices, 152-153
Juvenile delinquents, 265

Ladder of opportunity, 126, 127, 133
Latin, 186
Learning about the schools, 277-279
Length of education, 80, 85
Library, 153
Life adjustment education, 216-220
Limits on learning, 177-178
Local autonomy, 117-118, 292-293
Looky Finger, 264
Looky-Looky statements, 248

Masque and Gavel, 198
Master's degree, 246
Mastery of subjects, 17-18, 26-27
Mathematics, 19, 77-78, 78-79, 166
Mathematics Club, 162
Mechanical Drawing, 160
Minimum essentials, 56-59
Minority ethnic groups, 135
Missile race, 293
Model Airplane Club, 162
Multiple Causation, 10

Multiple curricula, 159
Multiple period organization, 165-166
Multisensory learning, 238
Multitrack curriculum, 285-286
Music, 151, 162, 163, 196
Musical instruments, expense to parents, 132

National Defense Education Act, 113-114
National Honor Society, 198
Necessary misbehavior, 76-77
Needs of youth, 148-149
New opportunities for folklore, 11-12
Nonrational behavior, 62-63
Normal differences in ability, 42-46
Normal schools, 101, 245

Occupational specialization, 71, 276
Orderly classroom, 67
Organizational revolution, 288-289
Orientation to teaching, 246

Pageants, 195
Panel discussions, 195
Parental responsibility, 70-71
Parochial schools, 119-120
Parties, expense to parents, 131, 132
Part-time employment, 83-84, 132, 168-169
Pay assembly, 130-131
Pedagogue, itinerant, 92-95
Personal and family problems, 218-219

Personality adjustment, 235
Physical education, 151, 160, 163
Physical examination, 36
Physics, 160, 209, 210, 211, 262-263, 286
Phonics, 12
Plane geometry, 160, 210
Practical science, 160
Private eyes, 220
Process and product in education, 28-31
Professional courses in education, 244-245
Professor Eminence, 248
Progressive Education, purposes, 227
Proms, expense to parents, 132
Psychology, 151
Public hearings, 292

Quill and Scroll, 198

Reading tests, 191
Red Badge of Courage, 21
Referral to family physicians and dentists, 36
Related mathematics, 160
Related science, 160
Reorganization of secondary education, 154-157, 217
Rifle Club, 162
Rockhounds Club, 162
Roles required of the teacher, 87
Russian education, 270

Satellites, 261
Scholarships and Fellowships Available at Institutions of Higher Education, 202
Scholarships, Fellowships and Loans, 202
Scholarships, 201-202
Science, 77-78, 78-79, 166
Science Club, 162
Science Fairs, 196-197
Science of education, 8-9
Secretarial curriculum, 160
Secretarial practice, 160
Segregated schools, 119-120
Separate school systems, 12-14
Separation of adult and child life, 11-12
Separation of curriculum from family and community living, 169
Separation of teachers from other adults, 81-82, 276
Shakespeare, 220
Shop mathematics, 159
Shorthand, 159, 160
Shy children, 62
Silas Marner, 21
Slow learners, 182-185, 188
Smith-Hughes Act, 113
Social conditioning, 139, 141
Social skills, 35-36
Social studies, 160
Sociology, 151, 160
Solid geometry, 160, 200
Special methods of teaching, 246, 247-248
Sputnik I, 261, 270, 274
Spelling, 39-40
Standardized tests, 15, 34, 44, 175-177
Stanford Achievement Test, 34
State aid to education, 111-112

State institutions of higher education, 24, 114-115, 126-127
Status, 51-53
Student teaching, 246, 254, 255
Subsidies, 202-203
Supplies, expense to parents, 129-130
Symbols of excellence, 240-242

Tale of Two Cities, A, 21, 99
Talking in school, 71-72
Taskmaster, 85-88
Tasks of American education, 281-283
Teachers colleges, 101, 245
Teaching aids, 238-239
Technical curricula, 158, 282
Tenth grade mathematics, 19
Tests and measurements, 246
Transcription, 160
Trigonometry, 158, 160, 200
Typing, 159, 160

Unification of learnings, 166
Units of credit, 151-152
Unnecessary talking, 71-72
Unrealistic concepts, 4-6

Variability of subjects, 21-23
Village apprentice, 95-97
Vocational agriculture, 215
Vocational curricula, 158, 160, 168, 212, 215-216
Vocational education, 113, 119

Weaknesses of professional education, 254-256
Whipping boy, 224-225
Work experience, 168-169
World history, 160
World problems, 160

Yearbook, expense to parents, 134